THE ROAD TO STRANGE
UFOs, Aliens and High Strangeness

THE ROAD TO STRANGE
UFOs, Aliens and High Strangeness

Michael Brein
and
Rosemary Ellen Guiley

Visionary Living, Inc.
New Milford, Connecticut

The Road to Strange:
UFOs, Aliens and High Strangeness

Copyright Michael Brein and Rosemary Ellen Guiley, 2018

All rights reserved.
No part of this book may be reproduced in any form or used without permission.

Front cover design by April Page Slaughter and Mark Stevenson
Back cover and interior design by Leslie McAllister
Main illustrations by John Weaver

ISBN: 978-1-942157-25-0 (pbk)
ISBN: 978-1-942157-26-7 (epub)

Published by Visionary Living, Inc.
New Milford, Connecticut
www.visionaryliving.com

Praise for *The Road to Strange: UFOs, Aliens and High Strangeness*

"*The Road to Strange: UFOs, Aliens and High Strangeness* is simply one of the best UFO books I've read in years. By that I mean a book which in one manner or another earnestly attempts to advance our understanding of UFO phenomena, the intelligences behind their breathtaking technology, and in the process, gives us yet one more real-world asset to recommend to anyone interested in furthering their own UFO-alien reality education. *The Road to Strange* accomplishes these objectives handily, but in a particularly methodical (and most appropriate) manner; that being, by respectfully, repeatedly, and deliberately delivering us into the lives of real people, one after another, as they each share an all-too-real memory a of life-changing sighting and/or experience.

"We shouldn't be surprised that this book is the outstanding UFO-literary powerhouse it is. Long-respected authors, lecturers, scholars, and world travelers Michael Brein and Rosemary Ellen Guiley remain highly focused throughout on delivering readers into these unvarnished, highly credible, firsthand witness and/or experiencer testimonies. Each one is followed by an appropriately thoughtful, insightful commentary, all of which reflect clear insights throughout.

"It's easy to allow things to get complicated when you're writing about the paranormal and UFOs, a challenge to keep things simple, even for the most experienced of writers, and Rosemary and Michael are writing at the top of their form. They make an old story come alive with new meaning, and they make it look simple. I among many others know from experience it is anything but. It is welcome to read both these authors again, and most appropriate that they chose to include selected parts of Brein's interview with UFO giant Dr. J. Allen Hynek. Dr. Hynek's words still ring out to us today in as timely a manner as when he first wrote them. Congratulations to the authors, and sincere thanks to all those good people whose accounts are included in this marvelous book."

– Peter Robbins, author and UFO researcher

"With the sudden, serious discussion of UFOs in a variety of mainstream media outlets, this ever fascinating—and important—subject has seen renewed attention. Many individuals have long worked to chronicle this unusual phenomenon; here, two of those researchers, Michael Brein and Rosemary Ellen Guiley, present us with some of the most perplexing and interesting cases that suggest the reality of unusual aerial phenomena in our midst. From sightings of enigmatic flying objects, to 'high strangeness' reports of incidents and occurrences that challenge the imagination, this collection of firsthand encounters lends a valuable sampling of case histories for review, as we look ahead to the future of UFO studies."

– Micah Hanks, UFO writer and researcher

Acknowledgements

We thank all of our contributors for their stories and illustrations, with special thanks to John Weaver for his original drawings; Ron Russell for his England experiences; Jacquelin Smith (website www.jacquelinsmith.com) for her human-alien hybrid views; and to Fatemag.com, Martin Jasek of www.ufobc.ca, and Lon Strickler's Phantomsandmonsters.com for providing archival background information.

Table of Contents

Preface by Michael Brein   xi
Introduction by Rosemary Ellen Guiley   xvii

"I Know What I Saw"
Something Was Watching Me · *Anita Sowles*   3
I Believe · *Valdo Viglielmo*   9
Punished for Seeing a UFO · *T.L. Murdock*   17
They Said It Was Squid Boat Lights · *David Crockett*   21
Confessions of an Airline Pilot · *Graham Sheppard*   25
UFO? What UFO? · *Various Authors*
    Complete Denial · *Chris Crispel*   31
    UFO Over Chicago · *Ellen Stuart*   32
    A Life-Changing Night · *Garry Sobek*   33
    Like Father, Like Son · *Dale Cox*   34

Mystery Lights and Craft
Flying Saucers Up Close and Personal · *Billy Vincent Pecha*   41
Chosen to Witness · *Norma Jean Conroy*   51
The Hole in the Sky · *Jayne S.*   57
UFOs in the Road · *Various Authors*
    The East Bay UFO · *Anonymous*   63
    UFO Hotspot in the Valley · *Anita Sowles*   64
Great Balls of Fire · *Colleen Hogan-Taylor*   69
Buzzed at the Zoo · *Kenneth Synnott*   73
Dancing With Angels … Or Not · *Angelica Chaparral*   77
Machu Picchu Magic · *Kristin and Jennifer Shotwell*   83
A Huge Red and White Triangle · *Maurizio P.*   87
UFOs Over Washington, DC · *George Wingfield*   91
A Sky Show in Kentucky · *Monte Val Stuart*   97
The Funny Lights of Guatemala · *Melo de Leon*   101
A Green Cigar and A Dark Shadow · *Charles Thatcher*   103

Sightings · *Various Authors*
    UFOs in the Nebraska Night Sky · *Steve Cosgrove*   107
    The Haleakala Lights · *Jerry Haile*   109
    UFO Over Medford, Oregon · *Robert Broberg*   110
    Strange Light Over the English Countryside · *Richard New*   110

Alien Encounters
The Road Trip Abduction · *Judy Kendall*   117
Pod Beings at Silbury Hill · *Ron Russell*   127
The Alien Examiners · *Mary Grace O'Meara*   135
The Grass-Eating Aliens · *Jeanine Taicher*   139
Abducted by Insectoids · *Jim G.*   145
Alien Machine Shop 101 · *Karl Petry*   157
A Night Like No Other · *Karen Lake*   161
The Borrego Springs Contact · *Norman Wayne Garcia*   167
An ET Visitor at Bowood Estate · *Ron Russell*   173
Human-Alien Hybrids on Earth · *Jacquelin Smith*   177
The Great White Brotherhood · *Rosemary Ellen Guiley*   185

High Strangeness
The Scorpion Portal · *Ron Russell*   195
Escapade at Area 51 · *Michael Brein*   203
Missing Time and Missing Exits · *Anonymous*   211
A "Phreaking" Man In Black · *Joey Madia*   215
Men In Black at the Library · *Joey and Tonya Madia*   219

Appendix 1: J. Allen Hynek on Extraterrestrial Visitation   229
Appendix 2: UFO and Related Organizations   233
About the Authors   235
Afterword   237

Preface
Michael Brein

I'm the "Travel Psychologist." I originally coined the term "Travel Psychology" during my doctoral studies at the University of Hawaii, and then became the world's first travel psychologist.

For five decades, I have crisscrossed and traveled the world many times over, interviewing nearly 1,800 travelers and adventurers, and collecting and recording more than 5,000 accounts of all sorts of things that happened to them. I have delved into the deeper psychological aspects of their experiences.

It became apparent during my research that many people got far more than they anticipated from travel – they had unusual experiences of a paranormal, supernatural, and even mystical nature. Furthermore, some travelers also had experiences of even more strangeness, including UFOs, aliens, crop circles and even MIB (Men In Black).

I saw common themes running through them. These stories fascinated me, and so I began a special collection of them, forging new territory in travel lore that had been ignored and neglected by the mainstream physical or social sciences.

Reading about the very high strangeness experiences of others presents the reader with new and unique events that are often both eye-opening and awesome – just as travel tends to be itself. It is largely through the novel experiences offered by travel and adventure that we achieve more personal growth and gain an understanding of realities that we perhaps did not know even existed. This aspect of travel is nothing short of a paradigm-shifter.

Travel is mind-opening and mind-bending. Maybe it takes the travel experience – namely the condensing, collapsing, and speeding up of time and space, the rush of novelty, all impacting upon us at once at every turn – to pry open the portals to the unknown. Imagine the degree of impact that a travel-related paranormal or even higher strangeness event can have on one's life. These events happen to everyone in all walks of life, regardless of belief in the paranormal or the strange.

Some of the people in this book acknowledge that they have personal and family histories of paranormal and other unusual experiences. That is the case with me, as I have had many episodes of premonitions, precognitive dreams, psychic phenomena, and some even of more strangeness throughout my life. I call this gift my "Inner Psychic."

Others in this book say they have no extraordinary psychic sense, and some even profess to be skeptical – that is, until their experiences open their eyes.

The stories in this unique collection are not intended to provide definitive proof of the paranormal or UFOs, or aliens, or Men In Black. My main purpose is to show that these kinds of experiences not only happen, but they happen often, and, yes, they happen to *you*, and to me, too! I have included paranormal experiences in our earlier book, the *Road to Strange: Travel Tales of the Paranormal and Beyond*, as well as a few of my own personal, highly strange travel experiences, which "seals the deal," so to speak, for the reality of psychic and other bizarre phenomena, at least for me!

The true stories presented here are a tantalizing mix of topics such as flying saucers, aliens, Men In Black, crop circles, space-time warps, possible UFO abductions, and considerably more. They take place in exotic locations all over the planet, and in all kinds of circumstances.

Reading these stories may help you understand some of the strange events you have encountered in your own travels – and may open you even more to the unknown and strange the next time you venture out.

Perhaps you have a high strangeness story yourself – see the information in the Afterword for how to submit for one of our upcoming volumes.

Before I go, I'd like to share a little more about how this book came into being, things deeply personal to me and which may very well involve experiences like the ones in the stories included here.

Preface

I'd like to describe how it is that the world's first *Travel Psychologist*, me, has become, in a matter of speaking, an *Alien Psychologist* as well, or perhaps stated in another way, an *Alien Ufologist!* Although I've never heard of such terms before, they do make sense in some way. Let me explain:

My involvement in the psychology of travel has led me to study the similarities and differences among peoples the world over. I've wondered, for example, what is the effect on people of travel to all sorts of exotic and fascinating places? And how do we change and benefit by doing so, and what effects do we have on peoples and cultures visited? Why travel? What is to be gained? What good is a better understanding that we could have from travel between ourselves and others?

The short answer is: a lot! Perhaps if we understand one another better, everyone can benefit by doing so, and wars and other conflicts might be reduced or eliminated entirely by simply coming to a better understanding and appreciation of one another. So, there is much to be gained.

Indeed, the study of the psychology of travel has also led me to explore further the implications of Earthlings' potential relationships with fellow beings from possible elsewhere and elsewhen. And one may ask even, after reading the stories in this book, "Well, isn't this possibly already happening here?"

The study of other intelligences, whether they have their own analogous forms of physical "flesh and blood," or whether they be ethereal or spiritual in nature, or even totally unrecognizable and possibly even incomprehensible to us, interactions that we may have in store for us with them demand a serious effort on our parts to understand them better. It may even be crucial to our survival as a species.

So, just who am I as a "ufologist?" A ufologist is a student of the subject of (U)nidentified (F)lying (O)bjects – UFOs – flying saucers! And as is the case with any field of human endeavor, it is but a single, tiny facet of all there is to know. As the saying from *The X-Files* television series goes, "The truth is out there," and with regard to the UFO, I, myself, am a seeker or collector of these truths.

As such, the ufologist is the collector of what truths are out there about these mysterious unknown flying objects flitting about our skies for hundreds, if not thousands of years, observed by millions of people around the globe, of all nationalities, persuasions and walks of life, including maybe even your mother, brother, grandpa, fellow office worker, your newspaper delivery boy, and who have you.

Don't just take my word for it, but I am convinced that UFOs are real. This means that they "exist" but what they are, well, who knows? They might be extraterrestrials (aliens), interdimensionals, future humans, cohabiting advanced earth species as yet unknown – it's anybody's guess. Perhaps the only way you'll be convinced like me is to have your own experience. Once that occurs, all bets are off.

The study of this subject has been, in my travel-life, a *raison d'être* for much of my travels. Armed to the teeth with a stack of unlimited free first-class airline tickets for a whole year (won in a United Airlines contest), what additional excuse did I need NOT to fly to all sorts of flying saucer conferences?

Well, I might as well have been a space alien myself, for I sometimes dropped right out of the sky to smaller, more local UFO meetings as well as larger ones around America. Of course, I didn't drop in totally unknown, for in all my involvement in the subject over the years, I've met just about every major researcher and speaker in the field, including my co-author, Rosemary Ellen Guiley. I have even been appointed as the "Ambassador-at-Large" for MUFON, the Mutual UFO Network – America's and indeed the free world's largest civilian scientific UFO research organization.

Suffice to say, that even though there is much humor and ridicule surrounding the subject of UFOs, I do have my laughs as well as my more serious moments. Please join me here in some of the humor as well as the import of my weird and wacky travels in the world of the UFOs.

I earned my PhD in social psychology. I have been fascinated with the subject of UFOs and the impact they have on people, and I tell everyone that if I had an office in a psychology department somewhere in a university, you'd see UFO books lining the shelves.

"Uh huh," say the naysayers!

Finally, I share the wonderment, the fascination and the quest for understanding of the experiences shared by the tellers of the stories in this book. Even some of my own earlier life experiences have led

Preface

me to be on my own *Road to Strange* in my search for answers and meanings to these mysteries.

Even back in my crib as a baby, I have the distinct memory of a green elf-like creature coming through the venetian blinds on my bedroom window and going directly into my clothing and toy closet. Alien? Fairy? Just an elf? Perhaps I'll never know. But I am sure this has had a profound effect on my desire to understand UFOs, aliens and other high strangeness.

And what moved me as a 10-year-old to read that famous 1952 Life magazine article, by H.B. Darrach, Jr. and Robert Ginna, on flying saucers and to conclude, *Geez, I think there really is something to this?* I was never quite the same after reading that article.

Some 50 years later, an army flight surgeon named Jesse Marcel, Jr. recounted to me his personal tale of how he, too, as a little 11-year old boy at the time, also had a momentous, life-changing experience and drew similar conclusions as I did.

His dad, Jesse Marcel, Sr., was the senior intelligence officer on duty at the famed Roswell Army Air Field base (RAAF) outside of Roswell, New Mexico at the time an alleged spacecraft crashed in the lonely, desolate desert plains of New Mexico in June 1947.

Jesse's father not only scooped up debris from the crash but deemed this finding so significant that he made a point to stop off at home in the middle of the night on his way back to the base and show both his wife and son that something very significant had just happened in the history of the world – that an alien spacecraft crash-landed and was about to be retrieved.

To this day, the U.S. Government alleges that no such thing ever crashed, and that there were other more prosaic explanations for what did take place on that fateful day.

But Jesse Marcel, Jr. maintains that he personally handled materials not of this earth, including "memory metal" that retained (went back to) its original state after you crumpled it, and an I-beam with strange, unearthly seeming hieroglyphics!

So, whether earth travelers have experienced, retold, and shared some of the highly exotic and strange stories about their own travels in these pages, or whether some of us earth people have had the chance to observe or interact in some way with the visits of highly strange, alien entities who are travelers to our here and now, we are all encountering one another together on that very self-same road – the *Road to Strange*.

> *"Thanks to Michael Brein… to be the pioneer of this field."*
> *– Shawn Koller, psychologist*

INTRODUCTION
ROSEMARY ELLEN GUILEY

Human beings have had encounters with visitors from other worlds and realities since our earliest documented history. We have many terms for them: angels, gods, fairies, extraterrestrials, interdimensionals, spirit beings, entities, descriptors (such as "grays" and "reptilians"), and proper names.

In this book, we have chosen to use "alien" (meaning foreign, unknown, strange, unfamiliar) as the broadest and most inclusive term, for in many cases – perhaps even in most cases – we really do not know exactly what we are encountering. We gauge what we perceive according to our worldview, background and even religious/spiritual beliefs, and our interpretations shapeshift over the years just as do the beings we are encountering. We do not know exactly where they come from. Do they arrive here from distant worlds, having found wormholes or portals or other ways to traverse the mind-boggling distances of outer space? Do they come from parallel dimensions linked to Planet Earth? Are they from the astral realm? All these explanations, and more, have been put forward.

What's more, what are the purposes of the aliens? Are they here to watch and study us, help us, save us from ourselves, warn us of impending disasters, trick us, manipulate us, enslave us, destroy us? All these explanations, too, have been put forward.

Hundreds of thousands of accounts involving UFOs and aliens have been documented, including sightings of mystery lights and craft; encounters with aliens ranging from puzzling to terrifying to rapturous; abductions; and a host of related paranormal and paraphysical phenomena that surround and trail these events, called "high strangeness."

This vast body of literature includes countless firsthand testimonies of eyewitnesses and experiencers. Eyewitness accounts are the gold of contact, enabling researchers to look into the mysterious depths of entity encounters for patterns and clues. In the early years of ufology, post-World War II, the primary emphasis was on "nuts and bolts" – hard physical evidence such as irrefutable photographs, pieces of craft or entire craft; and living or dead aliens. Such evidence would support the "Extraterrestrial Hypothesis" (ETH), that at least some UFO craft contain intelligent life from other worlds.

We are still in search of that evidence, though conspiracy rumors abound of caches of craft and even aliens, hidden away by governments who do not want the public to know that other-worldly beings are real – and here.

While some researchers cling to nuts and bolts as the only good evidence, most in the field have awakened to the importance of eyewitness testimony, even though it is subjective. Every day, the citizens of Earth have encounters with aliens. Probably most of them go unreported, for witnesses are, unfortunately, still subjected to immediate ridicule by experts, the media, and even their friends and families. However, more experiencers are coming forward, providing fresh material for researchers and databases that may provide insight into the mechanics and reasons of contact – and to the role of human consciousness, which may be the most important factor of all.

In this book, we have not attempted to duplicate the famous cases on record, though we do cite many of them for meaningful context in relation to other experiences. The stories are firsthand accounts of sightings of unexplained aerial phenomena, interactions with aliens, and unexplained paranormal phenomena related to UFOs and aliens. Most of the stories have never been published before, and they span more than a half-century in occurrence, right up to the present. Of those that have found their way into other outlets, the accounts are still fresh in the telling from the experiencers themselves, and sometimes with information and perceptions not related before. Almost all the stories are credited to the witnesses by name. In several cases, witnesses asked for anonymity or a pseudonym.

It is our purpose to acquaint the reader with the amazing range of activity involving UFOs and aliens concerning contact. We have positive, negative and neutral experiences. I have written commentaries at the end of the accounts to put the elements into perspective from the greater body of UFO and contact literature.

Introduction

Some of the experiences are part of what is called (lamentably) a "flap" in ufology, which is a sudden onset of intense or frequent activity that affects a specific geographical area. Flaps may be short in duration, or, like the Hudson Valley, New York black triangle sightings in the 1980s, go on for years. The informal definition of "flap" is "state of agitation" and "a panic," which in the early days of ufology might have been appropriate, especially since the skeptics were running the investigation show. It is a rather derogatory term today, in our opinion. Instead of flap, we have used "wave" to describe these periods of activity. If storytellers chose the term, however, we left it as is.

The book is divided into four sections and two appendices:

"I Know What I Saw" features witnesses who came forward with extraordinary stories and then faced a barrage of denial and ridicule, even from friends and family. Their experiences are sobering, especially if we put ourselves in their places.

Mystery Lights and Craft features the most common unexplained experiences: sightings of lights and craft in the sky, and landed craft. As you will note, many experiencers feel they were targeted to be a witness, and that there was an intelligence operating the lights and craft. Reactions range from fear to exhilaration.

Alien Encounters features accounts of direct contact with unknown beings. We include beings aboard landed craft, abductions, trips aboard craft, and spiritual experiences. Here again, humans react in a range of emotions.

High Strangeness features the odd phenomena surrounding UFOs and aliens: the mystery of crop circles; Men In Black; missing time; weird synchronicities; portals to other realities or timescapes; and other mystifying occurrences.

Appendix 1: J. Allen Hynek on Extraterrestrial Visitation features the visionary views of ufology's most famous researcher in an interview conducted by Michael Brein. J. Allen Hynek was way ahead of his time, and he had the courage – unlike some hardboiled skeptics – to change his mind about UFOs in the face of the evidence.

Appendix 2: UFO and Related Organizations gives the acronyms and a short history of major data collection and research organizations, so that we do not have to re-explain them throughout the book.

We raise and address many key questions about UFO phenomena and alien encounters. There is no doubt in our minds that nonhuman intelligent beings are real, and have been visiting Earth and interacting with people throughout our entire history.

In December 2017, the field of ufology was abuzz with the revelation that the Pentagon, at the behest of Congress, had spent about $20 million investigating UFOs – or "unexplained aerial phenomena," as governments now prefer to call them. The official purpose of the Advanced Aviation Threat Identification Program was to monitor any super-technology that might be developed by America's adversaries – but as ufologists and experiencers have known for decades, what we are talking about is no known Earth technology. The project examined scores of unexplained sightings by Navy pilots, military personnel and other observers of aircraft with capabilities far beyond what is currently considered aerodynamically possible. The sightings were often reported in the vicinity of nuclear facilities, either ships at sea or power plants. The study ended around 2012.

No one came forward to state definitively that the mystery craft belonged to aliens – but could such an announcement be in the not too distant future? If so, it would be confirmation for what thousands of experiencers already know: there is an alien presence on Earth.

We hope this book will be an enlightening companion to illuminate your own exploration of this fascinating mystery.

"I KNOW WHAT I SAW"

SOMETHING WAS WATCHING ME
Anita Sowles

A UFO overhead changes a woman's life in a profound way.

My sighting occurred in 1966 in Los Molinos, California, a small isolated rural area. My folks had a dairy farm there up against the foothills. There was nothing between the Sierra Nevada and us and on to Nevada.

The whole family one night observed a craft outside the dairy farm about a quarter to half a mile away, which had landed out in a field. We all went outside to look at this thing. It was sitting on the ground, and it was glowing.

The way this all started was that a little earlier on that evening, about dusk, my younger brother and a friend were on a motorcycle and were riding down a curving back road. Suddenly, they noticed a red light over the river about another mile or so away. My brother yelled to his friend, "Hey Mark, wouldn't it be funny if that thing came down?"

Anita is riveted by the sight of the huge craft. Credit: John Weaver.

Just as soon as he said that, that's exactly what happened: the object swooped down on the bike as they were turning the curve, and the bike spilled out, causing the light on the bike to go out. They were badly frightened. The thing lifted up at that point and flew off, and they continued home as fast as they could.

They burst through the front door of the old farmhouse while we were eating dinner. They couldn't talk coherently at all. At first, they stammered, they were so excited, and they couldn't quite get it together. They were both very emotionally uptight.

My sister, Kathleen, was visiting with us. My mother and father had just come in from the barn after milking the cows. My older brother was there as well. Everyone was seated around the dining table.

Kathleen was the first to run out the door to see what was going on and to determine what precipitated the terrified entrance of the boys. She yelled that there were five UFOs. We didn't actually call them UFOs at the time – we just said some "things," "craft," or whatever. They were buzzing the reservoir, which was right across the road from our house. We all followed suit out the front door.

By the time I came out to the front steps, the craft had lifted up and moved a little southward toward a grove of trees. I counted five of them hovering over the treetops. There weren't too many trees where we were, so they were clearly visible even though they were probably several blocks away by then. They were discs emanating a purplish glowing light. They were hovering over the treetops and just gliding along, doing what is often referred to as a "falling leaf" pattern of movement. At times they would bank at a 45-degree angle. The movements seemed to be casual.

I couldn't estimate their precise distance or size. They were fairly large in comparison to the treetops.

My brothers said, "Let's get in the van and go over there so we can get closer." They got in the van and took off to chase after the ones that appeared to be leaving. They drove about 15 miles or so, but never saw them or caught up to them. They gave up the chase and returned.

Unfortunately, they missed what happened next. One of the craft sped off from its new position towards Los Molinos and disappeared in a matter of seconds.

But it was not over! Almost instantaneously in the sky, a red light appeared directly above our house. Three other craft, including the one that I would soon see close up, came over nearby and hovered catty-cornered to our dairy house in the field belonging to our neighbors. It appeared to land there. It glowed a purplish reddish color and made a *wong-wong-wong* sound. Meanwhile, the remaining three other craft continued on their journey and disappeared in a southward direction.

At first, my father wouldn't come out to look at it, which left my mother, my sister Kathleen (who was holding her two-year-old daughter), my younger sister Terry, and me standing in our front yard watching what was going on. When he did finally come out he said, "Aw, government things!" He didn't believe that they could be UFOs, and went back in the house to finish his dinner. He would not budge from the table while all this was happening.

My mother was too frightened and had to go back into the house.

Then Kathleen said, "This thing gives me the creeps," and she also went back into the house and hid in a bedroom closet.

I stood out there by myself for 20 to 30 minutes. The craft rose off the ground and slowly moved towards me. It paused just over my head at about a 45-degree angle. I looked up at it and saw intense yellow light pouring out of what appeared to be windows all the way around it. What was really remarkable was that the whole bottom of the craft seemed to rotate in a clockwise direction, with red lights rotating around the entire craft. The original purple light had disappeared by now, leaving the entire coloring red and yellow. The light was too intense for me to see anything inside, and I don't think I could have handled it if I did. Yet I felt that something in there was observing me.

I became petrified. I ran towards the house. By the time I hit the steps, the craft turned on this high-pitched whirring engine sound that got to be deafening. It was gone instantly and soon became a single red light in the night sky.

I felt very insignificant. I felt the immensity of the universe, and before me, my small, insignificant world. All of a sudden, in my mind, enormous concepts of everything opened up and I felt so expendable, like I was the pet dog or even an ant, like we all are just one little speck in the universe.

The "Why me?" factor

After I got over the initial fright, I started being frightened all the time. It suddenly dawned on me, *Why me? Why did the craft wait?* It hovered 30 minutes or so until my mother was in the house and my sister was in the house in the closet. Why did it wait until everyone was gone and then come to me? I don't understand it.

If it did have an intention toward me, why did it allow me to run to the house? 'Cause I ran. It could have stopped at that point, or did "they" know that it would have been too touchy for me to see any more than I did? I definitely felt intention.

Evenings for me became bad. I was afraid to go to sleep. I was afraid it was going to come back and maybe take me away. I was having thoughts in my mind such as, *Okay, I need to go to sleep. When I go to sleep if you do come, this is private. If you do come, get me back by morning so that no one will know I've been gone. Don't let the rest of the family get hurt, or suffer because of me.*

The experience has stayed vivid in my mind for years, and it was years before I got over the anxiety.

I have wondered about abduction because of the time lapse with my brothers. We timed it from when my brothers took off in the van chasing after the UFOs, and by the time they came back, it should have only taken them about 30 to 45 minutes to travel that distance and come back. But it took them longer. Maybe abduction was involved with them.

Whenever I talked about the experience, I would be ridiculed and would be classified as weird. I had a very good friend. I tried to tell her, but before I could even begin, she'd start laughing. Finally, I said to her, "Okay forget it. I'm not telling anyone ever again."

She just didn't want to know. She'd say, "Oh yeah, you're really into that, aren't you?" Her husband was interested a little, so I told him, and she kind of listened in and said, "Yeah, you're really into that."

What she was saying, of course, was that she didn't believe me.

None of us discussed it much in public where anyone could try to discredit us. We didn't want to be called liars. But some of my family was there to support me. My father was very skeptical for years, but now he no longer is a skeptic.

Commentary

Many UFO experiencers feel that something intelligent aboard the craft is directing its attention at them, which can be a terrifying realization. They may feel that craft movements and the appearance of lights are done deliberately, as if "something" on board knows they are watching.

The ridicule that Anita and her family experienced is, sadly, par for the course, even after decades of reporting. UFO witnesses are treated as delusional. Even her own father, by refusing to participate, was in denial. He riveted himself to the table and his meal so that he could avoid dealing with – and even thinking about – what was going on outside.

It is common for eyewitnesses to shy away from hypnosis, because they do not want to be traumatized by more revelations, such as abduction or being transported aboard a craft. "Let sleeping dogs lie" is often the rule of thumb.

The case was investigated by Paul Cerny of MUFON (Mutual UFO Network), who helped Anita estimate the size of the craft in relation to the top of a large oak tree in the front of the property. Cerny said the craft might have been about 30 feet in diameter, which Anita felt was a good estimate.

I BELIEVE
Valdo Viglielmo

A man has two dramatic sightings in two countries, separated by 26 years, that convince him of the reality of UFOs – despite the denial of others.

Part 1

I was a student at Harvard at the time of the famous Kenneth Arnold flying saucers sighting in June 1947, which began the modern era of ufology. When a roommate of mine showed me the headline in a newspaper on June 25th, the day following Arnold's sighting, I had already heard something on the radio and people were talking about it. I was extraordinarily dismissive of it at the time, and I said something to the effect, "Oh, you know, this must be something else, and you can't believe that crap!"

But something happened to me in 1952 that changed all that. And, if that wasn't enough, later on, *again*, in 1978, I had an even more convincing sighting of a flying saucer. Two flying saucer sightings in a single lifetime! Because of these two incidents my life has never been the same.

In 1952, I visited relatives in northern Italy and then traveled by train on my way back from the Oriental Institute in Naples to Rome where my uncle lived. The train trip lasted about an hour. I was in a compartment with four or five other passengers, including several Italians and a German lady. This trip was about one month after the big UFO flap in Washington, DC, which was very much in the news at the time. I had been following it in the *International Herald Tribune*. There were sightings of UFOs over the White House, and the official explanation was a "temperature inversion." But many people felt that solid objects were even sighted on radar. Be that as it may, it was all abruptly dismissed by the authorities and media.

Suddenly the German woman started screaming, "Look out the window! Look out the window!"

We all looked out the window, and saw about five or six saucer shapes way in the distance at the foot of the mountains. Italy is very mountainous. We were looking to the east of the train, which was going along the Mediterranean coast. Thus, the mountains were on our right and the seashore was on our left.

I could tell, and everybody else could tell, that the objects were silvery metallic, reflecting the late afternoon sun.

I was baffled, utterly baffled! What I saw did look as if they were made by intelligent people, and that they appeared to be flying in a formation, almost like Kenneth Arnold's sighting of a flying formation of crescent-shaped UFOs over Mt. Rainier in Washington State.

The German lady screamed again, "They're coming from outer space! They're coming from Mars! Look, look, look, look!" She was absolutely hysterical, really frightened to death. She kept talking about the objects being from outer space, and they were coming to get us, and so forth.

I tried to calm her down. I said, "Yes, yes, very unusual isn't it!"

And then, because the train was moving opposite to the direction of the objects, and the objects themselves were moving off, they finally disappeared from view.

Honestly, I, too, was quite excited about it, and everyone else in the compartment seemed astonished and convinced that we had seen something very unusual.

It was a fantastic experience even though I didn't see them up close. In retrospect, because of the distance, I possibly could have easily talked myself out of it.

The following day, there was an article in the *International Herald Tribune* that reported that there had been many sightings exactly south of Rome where we were and had our own sighting on the train. I didn't report it myself, however. And I don't know if the hysterical German woman reported it, either. I don't know if anyone in the compartment reported it, but there were apparently reports, nonetheless, by other witnesses.

Part 2

After that sighting, and for years, I read all the UFO books I could get my hands on, including Edward Ruppelt's book, *The Report on Unidentified Flying Objects* (1956). I also read John G. Fuller's book, *The Interrupted Journey* (1966), about the famous Betty and Barney Hill abduction in New Hampshire, as well as Coral and Jim Lorenzen's series of UFO books. The Lorenzens started APRO, the Aerial Phenomena Research Organization, in 1952, in Tucson, Arizona, an organization dedicated to responsibly researching the UFO phenomena. There was also a very good article on UFOs in *Look* magazine at the time, read by a lot of people.

I continued developing a deep interest in ufology, to the point of boring my friends. There were people who said to me, "Val, we're worried about you." I was no doubt making a nuisance of myself with my friends, who really thought I was going off the deep end about it. To say the least, I was certainly obsessed with the subject.

I even read some of the junk stuff along with the good stuff, too. I was trying to sort out the wheat from the chaff.

Up through 1978, at the time of my second UFO sighting, there were peak periods of UFO sightings, called "flaps." In 1973, for instance, the Pascagoula, Mississippi UFO incident took place, where two fishermen were allegedly abducted into a waiting UFO craft and returned shortly thereafter.

There were lots of sightings in Hawaii at the time my wife and I arrived there to live in 1965. And there was a huge flap in the summer of 1965 all over the Midwest. Hundreds of thousands of people were seeing UFOs.

So, while I was preoccupied with the subject of UFOs, I also had other interests in my life: politics, and trying to do something to help people who were oppressed. I had always been somewhat left-leaning, politically, and I was involved in "People Against Chinatown Eviction" (PACE) in Honolulu, an effort to stop evictions of the poor and elderly that were taking place to make way for city revitalization.

One afternoon, I and some others attended a PACE meeting. My wife had the car, so I got there by my own steam, by bus. At the end of the meeting, I asked my good friend, Alan, "Alan, would you mind letting me bum a ride home with you?" I told him I lived in Aina Haina, a nearby suburb of Honolulu.

He replied, "Well, it's a little out of my way, but, sure, I'll do it."

So, there we were in his pickup truck. I was in the passenger seat and he was driving. As we drove, we were talking about what had happened at the meeting and what things we could do to get justice for these poor people.

To be sure, UFOs were most certainly not on the agenda, nor on our minds at all! For me they had certainly been on the back burner. Alan apparently had no knowledge, history or interest that I knew of on the subject. I had never brought it up with him.

On our way to Aina Haina, we exited the freeway where it ended and merged directly into Kalanianaole Highway. The time was about 6:30 PM and was dusk. The sky was starting to darken, but there was still some light.

I looked over towards the famed Waialae Golf Course, which was on my right. I noticed that the streetlights had just come on. But, oddly, I then noticed that there were two additional lights that were out of sync with all the others, which were spaced out in a line of streetlights.

Suddenly, the two out-of-sync lights lifted together right above the line of the other streetlights. The next thing I knew, they were *the headlights on a craft*, which started moving across the highway. That absolutely startled me.

These were *two* beams of light, exactly like the headlights of a car, maybe spaced three or four feet apart. They were the headlights of a very large craft that moved with no noise whatsoever about 20 feet above us, not even at treetop level. I did not see any windows. The craft spanned maybe 30 feet in diameter or 30 feet in length. It was *BIG, BIG, BIG!* As big as a house!

It then moved in a northwesterly direction across the highway, over the hills, in the direction of the island of Kauai.

All this all happened in the space of under a minute — maybe even 20 seconds or so at the point it passed us.

It was absolute bafflement! I thought, *This is happening to ME; this is happening to US! HAPPENING TO US!!*

Both Alan and I said exactly the same words virtually at the same time, "What the *HELL* was that?"

A few seconds passed; it was now already gone; we were stunned. I looked over at Alan and said matter-of-factly, "We have just seen a UFO!" I continued, "Well…? It's an object to me, Alan! It's flying! And it's not a helicopter! It's not a plane! It's *unidentified!* We have seen something that we simply cannot identify. That's all that means! It doesn't mean that it comes from Mars or that there are little green men in it!"

Alan said begrudgingly, "Oh wow! If you mean that. Yeah. If that's what you are talking about." He denied seeing it to the extent I had, which may have been the case since he was driving. But he did see it.

I saw it right from the beginning when it was still on the *makai* (ocean) side of the highway and it was hovering there. I saw it hovering, then it lifted up. We had the privilege of a 50-yard line view! We couldn't have seen it any better!

I don't know if anyone else saw it. I don't think there were any other cars approaching in the Honolulu direction while we were still on the ramp. And I don't remember seeing any other cars along with us going in our direction down the ramp.

I came home very dazed about it. I couldn't even talk about it for a while after the sighting.

It did not appear in the newspapers. Furthermore, I did not report it, nor did Alan.

Alan was upset and baffled. I think he wanted to instantly dismiss it, because what do you do with it? How do you fit it into your daily routine?

Every time I met with Alan after that – maybe 10 or 15 times at various meetings – I would try to talk to him about it. He'd say, "Yeah, strange, really strange, Val." And then he'd ask, "Have you done something with it?"

I'd say, "No, but I've probably talked to maybe 50 or 100 people about it."

I purposely didn't report it because I didn't want to get involved that way. I knew there was ridicule out there, and I didn't want to be ridiculed. I already had gotten ridiculed to some extent by telling some people about it.

For instance, I told one woman who was involved with us in our political activity, a very intelligent woman and a friend of mine. I told her the whole thing, and at the end of it all she said, "Val, it must've been a helicopter."

I said unabashedly, "You're out of your mind!" I even repeated, "You're out of your mind!"

I then thought about how the apparent government debunking campaign has been so successful. Think about it: I'm a believable person. I don't tell stories. I have a Harvard PhD. I'm as credible as they get. What the hell would I be doing making up such stories that might put me in the looney bin?

When something stupendous like this interrupts your life, it affects it. After my UFO sighting in Italy in 1952, I was able to get back to my normal life, because my sighting was at quite a distance. But with *this* sighting in 1978, I absolutely could not do that. I could *not* rationalize it away. The only possible way for me to do so would be if I had then seen a large secret craft of the United States or the Soviet Union – which I think is impossible, anyway. Why would they have a demonstration over a highway on Oahu in the Hawaiian Islands of all places? Why wouldn't they do it in Nevada or someplace else?

I did carry on with my normal life, teaching Japanese literature and being interested in politics. I still had many interests; and I had a young family – a young son and a daughter. But I became more intensely interested in reading about ufology, and I followed it from that point on to the present, picking up every book I could get on the subject. I think I've read a couple of hundred books or more on the topic.

There are dips and valleys in my interest. All things considered, I always return to this thing in 1978 and conclude unhesitatingly that something really, really *weird* happened.

Commentary

Countless witnesses like Val have the unpleasant experience of denial and ridicule on the part of others – even those who were also witnesses to the same event. No wonder that people are often reluctant to come forward; who knows how many events have gone unreported?

Witnesses who do speak up are criticized not only by their friends and family, but by the media, authorities, and other "experts" who do not know them or have firsthand evidence – but who are certain they are wrong. The most ludicrous "natural" explanations are often given instead.

In Alan's case, we do not know why he did not want to deal with the event. Perhaps it conflicted with his spiritual and cultural worldviews. Perhaps it was too "inconvenient" to have to contemplate the existence of alien craft and beings. Perhaps he, like Val, did not want to subject himself to ridicule.

Val was able to integrate both UFO experiences and further his exploration of ufology without derailing his life. Sometimes witnesses do become derailed, depending on the circumstances of the event, and the blowback from public scorn.

The fact that this event was not reported in the media does not mean it did not happen, or that it was "fantasy." There may have been others who either decided to remain quiet, or who passed it off like Alan. As many experiencers find – attested to in other accounts in this book as well – they are often the sole witness, for unknown reasons.

Ultimately, UFO witnesses are left to find their own personal meanings from their experiences. However, we share extraordinary experiences on a collective level too, so it is important for the information to find its way into the public arena.

PUNISHED FOR SEEING A UFO
T.L. Murdock

A young boy is beaten for telling his parents about a mystery light in the sky.

It was a spring day on a cotton farm in central Texas. The year was 1931 and the world was in the midst of the Great Depression. I was a four-and-a-half-year-old boy with many questions about the world I had been born into and no place to find answers. My hard-working parents were uneducated. I was the youngest in a family of six. My older sisters and brothers had no time for the questions of their kid brother. On this particular day, they were all on the far side of the farm chopping cotton. I was exempt because I was too young to use a hoe without chopping a foot off.

After a hard morning preparing the noon meal for her hungry brood, Mother would take a nap. Then she would get up and start all over again. I would help her in every way I could. And I was supposed to take a nap too, but I was much too restless. I quietly left the house and wandered out to my favorite sandbar to play with my one toy, digging in the sand.

On this particular day, the sky was full of beautiful, fleecy clouds gently moving and forming a multitude of different shapes. After tiring of digging in the sand, I lay back to watch the clouds. I could pick out a sheep here and a dog there, and – what was that! A cold chilly feeling engulfed me as a cloud moved over a round, shiny silver object, uncovering it to sky and sun. It remained stationary, for all the world to see like a great shiny eye staring down at me.

What was it? I knew about airplanes and Charles Lindbergh's flight. But airplanes were not round. How was it staying up there? I watched for a few minutes, transfixed. Then, suddenly, it shot up into the sky at a vertical angle and was gone from sight. I leaped up from the hole I had dug and ran to the house to tell my mom what I had seen.

She listened for a moment, then backhanded me full force for telling lies. Besides, I had been digging in the sand again and gotten my clothes full of dirt. There was no such thing as a round airplane; everyone knew that!

I left the house shedding tears of humiliation and frustration. I had been accused of lying when I was telling the truth. I hid out, waiting for my dad to come home from the fields – he would believe me. And maybe he could tell me what I had seen.

I was wrong. He got the razor strap and really gave me a beating for lying!

This experience had a bad effect on me for years to come. I learned that you could be punished and called a liar even when you were telling the truth. I never talked to anyone about what I had seen until something happened in 1947 that vindicated me. I was living in Chicago when I read an article that stunned me. An airline pilot had reported a fleet of nine round silver objects flying at great speed over Mt. Rainier in the state of Washington. I knew at once exactly what he had seen. In my mind's eye, I could clearly see once again the silver object hovering over the farm in Texas in 1931. The pilot's name was Kenneth Arnold.

After that, several people came forward with sightings. Many years later, I read that UFOs had been sighted as early as 1932 over Italy.

Why didn't anyone else see the same object that I did, you may ask. This was Texas in the 1930s, and there was little communication. No

TV and few radios, and only a bi-weekly country paper. This was about two in the afternoon and everyone was busy looking down at the young cotton they were thinning out. Others might have seen something but were afraid to comment. Look what happened to me!

As I have gotten older I remember it as clear as yesterday, what I saw hovering over me in that Texas field in the spring of 1931.

Commentary

Many children are reprimanded or punished for talking about their supernatural experiences: ghosts, angels, fairies, ETs, UFOs, mystery beings, and more. Adults tell children these experiences are "all in your head," or "it's your imagination," and warn them to "stop making things up," "stop talking like that," and so on. Some, like T.L. Murdock, are more severely punished, perhaps because such accounts conflict with religious views. Negative adult responses to the extraordinary experiences of children still happen today; they are not a thing of the past.

Children are more psychically open than adults in general. When their experiences are repressed or denied, they are forced to internalize them. The experiences may not stop, and so children then become at risk for fearing what they are seeing. Adults especially should pay attention to their children.

Even adults will deny what they have seen. They fear ridicule, or, their experiences contradict their religious or cultural worldviews, and they cannot cope with the implications.

Governments have been concerned about the effects of alien contact, and conspiracy theories that information is suppressed, and witnesses are discredited may have some basis in fact.

In 1960, the Brookings Institution issued a 186-page report for NASA, the National Aeronautics and Space Administration, titled "Proposed Studies on the Implications of Peaceful Space Activities for Human Affairs." The report discussed possible "disruptive" and "unpredictable" emotional and psychological effects of the discovery of superior life forms, depending on how the information was presented to the public. The report also discussed the withholding of information to the public as an option, but made no recommendations.

Governments are having a harder time holding their fingers in the dike, however. Witnesses have more opportunities to come forward than they did decades ago, with many publication options open to them, especially on social media on the Internet.

Nonetheless, automatic responses of skepticism and derision still kick in.

THEY SAID IT WAS SQUID BOAT LIGHTS
David Crockett

During the filming of a documentary of a prior UFO sighting over New Zealand, another UFO is sighted.

On December 21, 1978, the crew in a cargo plane flying over the Kaikoura mountain ranges in the northeast of New Zealand's South Island observed a series of strange lights that tracked along with their aircraft for several minutes before disappearing and then reappearing. They saw a large UFO with five white flashing lights.

After this dramatic sighting, I was part of a news crew from Australia that was asked to go up in an aircraft and film footage for a documentary reenactment. We took off on December 31. We had no idea that we would encounter the real thing.

We were over the west coast of the South Island of New Zealand. We were not very high out of Wellington, which is in the lower half of the North Island, when the pilot of our aircraft called us up to the flight deck to say that he had some objects or bright lights off the coast of Kaikoura, a little township just down the coast.

We completely forgot about what we were doing, the fact that we were there making a documentary, and went up onto the flight deck. I tried desperately to capture these things on film, but, looking through the viewfinder of the camera, they seemed to be too far away to be very clear or to be able to be picked up on film.

This was the start of quite an exciting and frightening night, because we had numerous sightings all the way down the coast for about 200 miles from Wellington to Christchurch.

Because of this immense activity, the pilot of the aircraft invited us to come back on the flight deck on the homeward leg back up to Blenheim. It was good that he did, because it was on this particular leg of the trip that we saw a tremendous bright light, which now is known as the world famous "New Zealand UFO," or the "Kaikoura Lights."

The experiences that everybody had on board were really quite frightening. We were flying towards this object and having the radar people say that it was also traced on the radar screens. And when we turned towards it, it came up on the aircraft radar screen. It was all very scary.

One reason why we were frightened was the recent disappearance in October 1978 of a plane in connection with a UFO. The afternoon before we went up on this flight, we'd been discussing the incident that took place in Australia, which happened to pilot Frederick Valentich over the Bass Strait, between the mainland and Tasmania. Valentich was piloting a small, light aircraft, and he was continually being buzzed by a bright object, similar to the one we saw. He radioed to the control tower to say that this thing was not an aircraft and was buzzing him and coming towards him. Finally, there was a metallic sound and sort of a crash, and they never heard anything more. They couldn't find any trace of him. He completely disappeared – plane and all.

When we were heading towards this unknown object ourselves, everybody was very aware that this same sort of thing might happen to us. Even the pilots, who had about 26 years of experience, were disturbed, and had discussed leaving the flight home until the next morning. They did not, fortunately, or we would not have seen this UFO.

On the return trip from Blenheim, we were at about 20,000 feet when we encountered a giant light that settled near a wing and tracked us for about 15 minutes – and we were able to film it.

I think everybody on the aircraft had a strange feeling. It was as if a strange atmosphere fell over the whole aircraft. When it struck me the most was when I was about to change the lenses on my camera. I realized that the 240-mm lens, which I wanted to use, was in the camera case down in the back of the aircraft, where we had left it. To get to it, I had to go down the flight deck stairs and climb over the freight and this tremendously huge flight deck. It was quite dark, and to know that this UFO object was just outside the aircraft – I just couldn't get back up with the other people quickly enough. It was quite an effort.

When I put the 240-mm lens on and put it up to the window of the aircraft, it was the most thrilling thing that I've ever seen through a camera – and I've been filming for 20 years or more. When I focused the lens I saw this oval object with vibrating rings spinning around the outside of it!

It never ever came out on film the way I saw it through that viewfinder. It was just an amazing sight, and I can remember saying to the reporter who was with us at the time, "These vibrating spinning rings are on the outside as though it is some sort of field traveling around this object."

I also felt there was a presence, something in the aircraft as well, something surrounding us. It was intelligent. The UFO either had somebody in it or was being operated from some source that we don't know about.

When the film was developed, we saw that in one frame this object did a tremendous sort of figure-eight. There is no way that the camera movement alone could have done that. So, it was this object that did that. It was estimated to have done this leap in a speed of about 14,000 miles per hour. What machine made on this earth can go that fast?

This experience affected my life tremendously, and I became immersed in UFOs. About four or five days after this incident, I decided to make another documentary film, for many reasons. One of them was that I thought newspapers had got the wrong idea about the whole thing. They thought we were up there *chasing* UFOs, which was completely wrong. We were there purely to make a reenactment documentary about a previous sighting.

So, I decided this film had to be made. I financed the whole thing myself. I created a complete and accurate record of what happened that night: the experiences of everybody. I've traveled around the world to spread the word.

I'm not trying to convince people about UFOs, but tell them the truth of what happened then, and to try to get high government people more interested in the aspect of what's happening in our skies. I think it's essential that scientists take a serious look at this phenomenon and try and figure out what it is that's there.

I agree with Dr. J. Allen Hynek, who said this was probably not the most spectacular sighting, but it certainly was the most well-documented sighting up to that time. We had five people on board the aircraft who witnessed the UFO; we had radar returns from the aircraft when it turned towards us; we had radar tracking from the International Airport at Wellington; and we have it on color film. There are over 30,000 picture frames of this object to analyze.

Commentary

The New Zealand UFO still remains one of the best-documented sightings in ufology. Despite the dramatic film footage, the witnesses were ridiculed and "experts" jumped in with denials and ridiculous explanations. An investigation was conducted by the Royal New Zealand Air Force, the police and the Carter Observatory in Wellington. The New Zealand Ministry of Defence explained away the lights as the planet Venus, meteors, lights from trains and cars, and, most amazingly, lights from squid boats that reflected off clouds.

Dr. Bruce Maccabee, an optical physicist and former research physicist at the U.S. Naval Surface Warfare Center, examined the film footage and said it was authentic.

CONFESSIONS OF AN AIRLINE PILOT
Graham Sheppard

A former British Airways captain has two inflight UFO experiences and comes face to face with an anti-UFO work climate.

First UFO Encounter

In March 1957, I was one of three on the flight deck of a Vanguard aircraft on a flight from Gibraltar to London, a trip that takes about an hour-and-a-half. It was a routine run that I'd done many times before. It was winter, and the sky was completely clear – a beautiful starlit night.

Around 8:30 at night, we were north of the Bay of Biscay, and we noticed up ahead a "star" that was not on our star chart. It was suddenly brilliant – very, very bright. It was completely stationary in the northern night sky. We thought it was odd, and we looked at it for a long time.

Then it started moving from right to left, and descending and changing color. It started aerobatting, that is, making figures of eight, looping the loop, all at very high speed. Then it was joined in an instant by another bright light – there were two of them doing these maneuvers. All three of us were extremely interested, and kept watching.

We checked with Gibraltar radar and asked if they had any trace of these objects. They said, "Yeah, we've got unidentified traffic out to the west side."

I don't think any of the passengers noticed this, as the lights were straight away ahead of us. There was no way they could have seen anything.

For the rest of the flight, the three of us discussed it, and we thought it was so unusual that we should put in a report.

Normally, by the time we get back after a long day or a long couple of days away, we run to our cars to get home. But on this night, after we got back to London, we sat down for a long time talking about what we were going to do.

The skipper was quite adamant. He said, "You must not report this! It will affect your career and it will have an imperial effect on your progress in the airlines." It was quite clear that his warning was based on knowledge. I also had the impression that it was some sort of spillover from the military, and we needed to keep these things under wraps, especially on the civilian side of aviation. So, we did not report it.

At the time, this was an unusual experience for pilots. But as the years went by, the feeling became – and here's where the debunkers have been so successful – that UFOs had become a wacky subject. Pilots are supposed to be ultra-rational; they should not have an interest in a wacky subject like UFOs! That also applies to all "wacky" subjects – anything that would be considered out of the norm for a pilot.

It wasn't just my airline – this attitude was pervasive throughout the industry.

Nonetheless, for years I tried to bring the subject up into conversation with the flight engineer, or whomever I flew with. I was always the only one to bring the subject up, and if I did, I would get no interest, even though I knew other pilots and flight engineers had seen UFOs. I have never flown with another pilot who actually introduced the subject into a conversation. Never.

At the time, I chalked it up to the success of the debunkers. It wasn't so much that UFOs had to be a deep dark secret – it was nobody wanted to be a "wacky" pilot. It would be death to your commercial career.

I just wanted confirmation that we are not alone on this planet.

This experience kindled my interest in UFOs – but it was not my first experience. When I was 11 years old, growing up in Pembrokeshire, Wales, I had a UFO sighting.

Second UFO Encounter

Then in the 1960s, I had another UFO experience while flying, this time in daylight. We were on an international flight from Scotland to London. It was perfect flying weather.

When we were over the Midlands of England we got a radar alert about an object traveling at high speed directly in the airway. We saw this disc coming towards us! It was about 30 feet across, and it looked as if it was going to come extremely close to us.

You don't have time to be worried in situations like this – you have to react according to your training. This object was going very, very fast. It came past on our right-hand side, and I was able to look down on it. It was indeed disc-shaped, like a discus.

I thought, *This is a flying machine from somewhere else!* I had no doubt.

All of us in the cockpit looked in surprise at each other.

Officially, we passed it off to something explainable, a vehicle from somewhere else on Earth that we did not know about. That was our ultra-rational training kicking in.

At the time, there was a lot of UFO activity all over England being reported from people on the ground. I remember the police in Devon chasing things all over the place, and there were lots of articles in the press.

Nowadays, is seems that more people who look out of airplane windows, including passengers, see unexplained lights and craft. Don't sit there and do crossword puzzles – look out of the windows!

It's funny, nobody hardly ever looks at the sky. People come out of the bars and go straight to their cars. They're busy looking for their keys to get into their cars and they never look up at the sky. Nobody looks up at the sky!

I think these things are powered by beings from somewhere else. They can mix and match; they can move in and out, not only in their own space-time in real terms, but they can move in and out of our reality at will. I think they have stealth technology that moves from the visual spectrum to the radar spectrum and beyond.

Commentary

The reporting climate has changed considerably since the times when Graham Sheppard had his experiences. More pilots have come forward about their sightings and even close encounters with craft; however, fear of career backlash still exists.

In 1999, Dr. Richard Haines, former chief scientist at the NASA (National Aeronautics and Space Administration) Ames Research Center, founded NARCAP, the National Aviation and Reporting Center on Anomalous Phenomena, to collect such information from airline professionals. The organization has collected thousands of reports, which probably are a small tip of the iceberg.

Pilots have contended that it is "beyond dispute" that pilots encounter UFOs. In 2013, pilots were among those who spoke up about their experiences at the Citizens Hearing on Disclosure at the National Press Club in Washington, DC, at which UFO testimony was given to six former members of the U.S. Congress, to advocate public disclosure.

Some pilots who inform their superiors of their experiences are still told to never talk about them publicly.

Speaking at the Washington, DC, hearing, commercial pilot Jim Courant told about a pilot who was flying a 747 over the Pacific Ocean in 1980, and spied a UFO in front of him that was bigger than his plane. The pilot reported the sighting after landing in Japan, was debriefed, and told never to mention it again.

The Internet and social media make it much easier for such stories to leak out, although according to Courant, some pilots keep quiet because they fear consequences, not only for their careers but also for the safety of their families.

One of the most famous commercial pilot sightings occurred in 1986. Japan Airlines Flight 1628 was on a special flight carrying French wine from Paris to Iceland and the United States via the Arctic Circle. While over Alaska, Captain Kenju Terauchi noticed lights to the left and right of his airplane. At first, he thought they were U.S. border patrol planes flying along the U.S./Soviet Union boundary. But the objects reappeared very close to his plane.

He described two objects as square "spaceships" with jet propulsion systems that had horizontal lines of circular exhausts around a dark center. They fired off exhaust, seemingly to keep their craft in balance. Terauchi had the impression they were controlled automatically. He also noticed interference with his ground communications, a jamming that sounded like "zaa, zaa." The two square ships were joined by a third object, shaped like a walnut and the size of an aircraft carrier.

Terauchi and his two crew members watched the lights for about seven minutes when suddenly two spaceships stopped in front of their plane, shooting off bright lights that lit up the cockpit and even created a sensation of warmth on Terauchi's face.

The objects were caught on radar at the Air Route Traffic Control Center in Anchorage, Alaska.

Terauchi did not fare well in the aftermath. Officials said he was "overly eager" to describe the lights as spaceships, and that his testimony did not match the communications with the Federal Aviation Agency's (FAA) ground controllers. To make matters worse, his copilot and flight engineer said the objects were just "lights."

The FAA concluded there was no hard evidence to substantiate Terauchi's claims. Civilian skeptics said Terauchi had seen nothing more than light refraction through ice crystals suspended in clouds.

Squid boat lights, anyone?

Meanwhile, Graham Sheppard went on to have a dramatic spatial displacement in March 1993 while flying a Cessna 172 from San Juan to Mayaguez, Puerto Rico. He told ufologist Timothy Good about it, and Good included it in his book, Unearthly Disclosure (2000). According to Good:

> Shortly after overflying the Arecibo radio telescope, he [Graham] suddenly found himself 25 miles to the south, and about to infringe on restricted airspace. On two occasions, in 1998 and 1999, Graham and I hired the

same plane to fly the same route, but we were unable to come up with a conventional explanation.

"In 14,000 hours of flying worldwide, I have never experienced such a bizarre and unnerving incident as this one," wrote Graham.

In 1994, Graham Sheppard retired and in 1995 made his first public appearance to a large audience about his UFO experiences at the annual Ozark UFO Conference in Eureka Springs, and was well received by the audience.

He passed away in 2005, but his testimonial remains on the records. In his eulogy, Timothy Good described Graham as "the consummate pilot's pilot."

UFO? WHAT UFO?
Various Authors

To tell others or not about a flying saucer sighting is a tough issue for some, as these accounts demonstrate.

Complete Denial
Chris Crispel

A youth gets a rude shock after he and a buddy see a UFO.

In 1956, I was in high school. I returned home with my best friend Alan after a day of misery in school. The bus left us off about a quarter of a mile from our homes. I looked out and saw a bright disc in the sky, in full daylight, at about 4 PM.

It traversed the sky from one end to the other in a matter of seconds. We were both astounded and shared ideas about what it could be, i.e., sun spots, flying saucers, etc. When we went home, we told our mothers about it.

My mother listened intently, and she said she believed me about the experience I had. She was not humoring me; she truly accepted my account of the incident.

However, the next day, my dear friend said he saw nothing! I presume his mother told him not to ever tell anyone about it, because they would think him crazy. He never recanted, and years later told the same story of never seeing anything.

UFO Over Chicago
Ellen Stuart

A UFO buff, trained as a field observer, has her own sighting but runs into denial.

Right before lunch on Wednesday, August 30, 2006, I was sitting at my desk and looking out my office window. The window was eight feet away from my desk, and looked out in a southeast direction from Lake Michigan toward U.S. Cellular Field. Suddenly, I thought I saw a UFO!

The object was shaped like a UFO, with no visible wings, and it was over the building that obstructed about two-thirds of the view of the sky from my window.

Out loud I said, "What is that?"

I went over to the window. I then called the lady who sat next to me to look at this object with me. Both of us watched as it "floated" to the right, went behind the tower that sits atop the building we see through the window, emerged on the other side of the tower, continued moving to the right in a mostly horizontal direction, and then diminish in size. We lost the object as it became too small to see in the gray, cloudy sky. I estimate we had about 30 seconds total in sighting time.

The object was fat in the middle and tapered on the sides, and had a yellow hue. Its main characteristic was that it moved as though it were floating on water. It did not ascend very much as a balloon would have done. We could discern no wings.

Later I took out my ruler and measured that the object appeared one-quarter-inch to one-half-inch in size at arm's length. We surmised that when we first saw the object, it was probably over Soldier Field. It moved in the direction of U.S. Cellular Field.

As I am a trained field investigator for MUFON (Mutual UFO Network), I am familiar with UFO shapes and ways they move, which is why I quickly mentally ran through the list of identifiable possible objects (plane, blimp, bird, balloon, etc.), eliminated all of them, and felt rather certain, especially because of the way the object floated as though it were on water, that it was probably a UFO.

The lady who saw it with me did not "believe" in UFOs, and each time I related this sighting to fellow workers, she maintained that she could not identify the shape or explain the way it moved, and said she had never seen anything like it.

A Life-Changing Night
Garry Sobek

A skeptical man has a life-changing UFO event that takes place high in the nighttime sky right above him.

In 2013, I was outside one night on my deck on Bainbridge Island, Washington, at about 9 or 9:30, looking up at the beautiful sky in no particular direction, but pretty much just straight up. I was trying to pick out the constellations and things like that, and I happened to see something moving oddly. I've seen the space station go by before many times, but this was much further out than the space station.

It was moving at what I thought was a very high speed, and was nothing that the U.S. military or science community would own.

Then I saw it make a turn that defied all physical reality – the sharpness of the turn. Then a second light object of about the same dimness and same size joined it, and they were going in a kind of a parallel pattern and making these turns that were just hard to believe. They seemed to slow down a little bit before they went into their turns, but the turns were just physically beyond comprehension. They were so sharp, not quite 90 degrees, but arcs.

I kept watching and watching it as long as I could, until they made a straight line out of my field of view hidden by a tree. I was so blown away by then. To see an asteroid or meteorite going at a high rate of speed reflecting light is one thing, but to see objects make the kinds of turns that these two objects were making was pretty awe-inspiring.

I called my wife to come out to see it, but by the time she finished up whatever she was doing, they were gone. This probably lasted a total of a minute or maybe 90 seconds.

Who knows what it was, but it certainly wasn't anything that I've seen in my last 60-plus years on this planet. If it was something that was from another country or military on this planet, it's certainly top secret. But I think they were probably something from another world. I stayed up half the night talking about it to my wife, it had so profoundly affected me.

There's a social stigma about talking about UFOs, because most people think you're "out there" and whatnot. But the reality is I saw this with my own eyes and I know what I saw! I'll leave it at that. In my personal opinion, there seems to be a government cover-up to not be transparent with the general public regarding these kinds of events.

Like Father, Like Son
Dale Cox

A father and son both have their own separate UFO sightings years apart.

1. "Don't Talk About It!"

In the spring of 1942, my father, Victor Vivian Cox, had just started working his way up in his career with a transit company. One day, he and his two friends, Bill Richardson and Bill Lindsey, were out on their lunch hour golfing on the East Moreland golf course, in Portland, Oregon.

It was a clear day, and suddenly this item, or whatever it was, came right out of the sky – a brilliant orange-like flaming, tubular, cylindrical thing. It was covered with almost like a brilliant orange flame. It just came down from the sky to about 30 to 40 feet off the ground.

It was vertical. As they stared at it, a little ladder-like thing appeared, as though dropped from the bottom of the thing. It did not touch the ground. The thing held there for about 10 seconds or so, and then it simply lifted up and took off!

Both Bill Lindsey and Bill Richardson admired my dad because he was coming up through the ranks of the chain of command and he was darned smart at what he did. They looked up to my father because he had already shown great ability to lead.

They said, "Vick, what do we say?"

All my dad said was, "Do you like your jobs?"

"Well, sure."

"I'd say nothing!"

They never talked about it again, and my father did not speak of it until after he retired in 1980. He said he knew UFOs had been around for a long time, but you couldn't talk about them.

I said, "Dad, why is the government so apprehensive about the phenomenon of UFOs?"

He just stared at me and said, "Do you want the short answer?"

"Well, yes sir."

"Two things: the stock market and loss of control of the public, in that order!"

That was all he would say.

2. "Please Tell Me What I'm Seeing!"

In the fall of 1970, about 5:45 PM in the afternoon, I was going home on the Bainbridge Island Ferry on the way back from Seattle to Bainbridge Island. Some of my fellow staffers and architects were there with me, and we were having coffee. It was a very cloudy fall day with no rain.

I looked out one of the ferry windows and saw this huge hemispherical silver thing steadily moving through the sky northward. I could tell it was real because the cloud formations were reflecting off of it. It was so big. It was huge. The thing must have been almost as big as a football field, and it was going steadily north over the Magnolia Bluff area of Seattle.

What really got me was that I could not get anyone to look up from what they were doing, including one of my colleagues who was brilliant at architectural design and had his masters in architectural engineering. He wouldn't look up at all from what he was doing.

Wanting some kind of acknowledgement or confirmation, I said, "Will somebody look up at the window and tell me what I'm seeing!"

One of them even said without looking up, "Oh, Dale, maybe it's a UFO," and then he just went back to his crossword puzzles!

The object disappeared into the clouds. No one else around me gave any indication that they had seen this thing, too. There wasn't anything about it in the newspapers.

I guess that's the way some people are – they won't look up.

Commentary

Sometimes the most difficult aspect of a sighting is grappling with whether to tell others, and risk being called a liar, lunatic or worse. "I know what I saw" has become a mantra for witnesses facing a barrage of debunking, criticism and ridicule.

Experiencers often are not surprised to be derided in the media, but it really stings to be repudiated by a friend or family member who shared the experience, as Chris Crispel noted in his story.

On January 8, 2008, the farming and ranching community of Stephenville, Texas became ground zero for a dramatic UFO sighting. The yellow-red lights, seen by multiple witnesses, flashed and moved into lines and arcs. Up to 9 or 10 lights were seen. The local airport and Fort Worth control tower said nothing was flying. The military denied having aircraft in the area, then said the lights were flares dropped by military planes on training maneuvers.

MUFON (the Mutual UFO Network) became involved in the Stephenville investigation. Soon eyewitnesses were backbiting each other, claiming some stretched their stories to get attention, or had no credibility. Some cast aspersions on the motives of MUFON, and complained about how the media portrayed them as hicks and nuts. "I made the mistake of saying it [the UFO] was as big as a Wal-Mart," eyewitness Steve Allen said. "People have been teasing me about it ever since."

A powerful undercurrent of fear, denial and ridicule has always plagued the UFO field. Researchers, the public and the media clamor for evidence and personal accounts – and then immediately leap upon them to discredit them.

Fortunately, experiencers continue to come forward, and many quietly find support groups and communities of like-minded people who are more interested in finding the meaning of their experiences than in proving them to skeptics.

MYSTERY LIGHTS AND CRAFT

FLYING SAUCERS UP CLOSE AND PERSONAL
Billy Vincent Pecha

A quiet late evening is interrupted by several huge flying saucers up close and personal, complete with disturbing effects.

I lived in a small trailer house out on the edge of the town of Colusa, California. I had my workshop there as well. On the night of September 9-10, 1976, at around 11:30 PM, I had just taken a shower and sat down on my living room couch to watch a late movie on TV. My wife, Dede, and children were already in bed. My wife had fixed me some coffee, so I told her I was going to watch a little TV and go to bed later. I wanted to unwind a bit before going to bed.

      Suddenly, at around 12:30, the TV began to go haywire. I muttered to myself, *Darn, whatever this is, it has interrupted my favorite TV program.* The TV went on and off, and it would seem to lose power. Also, the picture would shrink down, too. I thought it must have been the tube finally going on the blink; it was probably long overdue to happen.

My air conditioner-cooler kept going down real low as well, as if it was going to lose power. Then it came back on normal and was pretty good for a few minutes. But then it just went real slow again, this time making a weird *squeeching* sound. Finally, it completely died on me. I thought, *What the hell has happened now?*

So, I raised myself up off the couch and looked out the window towards my shop and noticed that the night light wasn't on. I figured that the circuit breaker must have probably tripped, and I had better go out and see what I could do about it. Since I had my shorts on, I went tippy-toe along the house so as not to be seen by anyone in the neighbor's house. I intended to simply flip the switch and get right back to my program.

As I got my feet on the grass I began to feel an odd little electrical tingling effect. I thought, *Well, maybe the thing shorted out in the ground somewhere in my setup for watering the lawn.* It got awful hot over here in the valley, so there was constant watering taking place.

As I was approaching close by the bedroom window where my wife was sleeping, my hair started raising up and crackling, and I felt a little more sensation of a shock. It worried me; I didn't know whether I should continue to step in that area or go back the other way. I was thinking, *Wow, I really got a good short here!*

It started getting strangely more and more quiet. It was hot and sticky – a little sultry with the temperature in the high 90s. I noticed it was a full moon, and it was very bright outside and eerily very still.

When I reached the end of my trailer house, I could see this very odd dark shadow on the ground by my house, so I instinctively looked up, because I figured there were clouds coming or something casting this odd shadow. I thought, *What could it be?*

Incredibly and beyond all belief, there was this huge flying saucer hovering mostly over my barn and partly over my trailer house. It was about 50 feet in the air and completely silent, and was beaming down from its center a dull gray purply light. What was strange was the light only came part way down. I was really petrified by what I was seeing.

There were six rope-like cables hanging down. The three on one side of the craft were hanging down at different lengths, with the longest one almost touching the roof. The three cables on the other side, however, were all hanging down evenly. The cables came off the edges of the craft. All of them were frayed, like steel cables that have been pulled apart at the ends and then splayed outwards. There were two pincher-like appendages. I was afraid, thinking that the cables were some sort of sensor.

An outer rim rotated slowly around the outside of the craft.

This thing was so electrifying that my hair was beginning to stand up on my arms as well as everywhere else. In fact, my hair even crackled for a second.

The only sounds I heard were *snap, snap, snap, click, click*.

Most people would have surely run in fright, but I stood out there taking this all in, perhaps mesmerized by it all.

Since it was a bright moonlit night, with the full moon reflecting off this thing, I could begin to make out details. In the reflection, I could see a powdery blue haze on my arms. I was really getting frightened. In fact, I was trying to holler to my wife, but I couldn't get anything out. I had my mouth open, but nothing would come out.

Now, I could start seeing all the features of it real good. I was looking up at the edge of it. I started walking a little closer to it and I got right up underneath it, just inside and under the edge, a big shadow was underneath, and the light that shined down was fairly dim and grayish with a purplish tint.

A big spinning rim appeared to be "sandwiched" in between the top and bottom discs. It was spinning very slowly. Everything about it was still, except for the rotating rim.

Up inside was this beautiful finish. It was like ceramic. It was kind of silvery, but still it was an off-white; the upper half was more silver. I don't know if it actually was silverish because the moonlight was on it. In the center was a huge deep hole with a dim purplish-grayish kind of light up inside. I could see deep up inside there. It was definitely dark.

As I walked closer to the craft, the arm things tucked up and the cables followed suit, going up very fast. The cables were hanging out of what looked like hole fixtures, but when they retracted there was nothing there, not even holes for the cables to fit in.

"They" must have known I was there, because nothing much was happening until I got up under the craft, and it started doing things and began eventually to back away, like either they didn't want to be seen or they had already seen *me* before I even got out of the house.

I didn't think about trying to communicate with them – I was too scared. All I could think about was protecting my family and shooting at it, but I never got close to the gun once I got to the house. After I had seen what it was doing, I didn't think a gun would have done any good. The greatest power over me at the time was fear about saving my family and getting out of there, and that was it.

I was under the craft for at least a good six minutes. Then it started rising very slowly, and out from the center portal came a light like a sealed beam. On the top end of it were these clusters that looked like sugar cubes or flash cubes.

The thing began to slowly back out, moving toward the crop dusting field on the neighboring ranch just in back of me. It started pulsating brightly and the center light now came on even brighter.

New lights on arms came out from the sides and swept back and forth in a circular motion across that field, as if searching for something. The truncated light beam from the center of the disc now started to come down straight to the ground. At first, the light beam had only come down about halfway to the ground. It was as if somebody had simply cut it off with a knife.

As it backed out, the dome became more visible. I could make out the top by then. The top and the bottom discs were concave dishes. The craft had been at an angle when I first walked under it.

Behind this craft I could now see two more like it, one on each side, about half the size of the main ship. I didn't notice them at first, because I couldn't see them. And that's when I started thinking, *Well, this must be it for me!* I became real afraid. I mean, I was already scared, but now I figured, *Well, there's something really bad going to happen.* I thought about getting my rifle.

Then the three ships moved back toward my neighbor's house (John W. "Slim" Davis), which was a good quarter of a mile away. Just then the main craft dropped a light from its center over the top of my neighbor's house. It got real bright, like a phosphorus flash cube light, and it stayed on that way.

It not only lit up their two-story house – I could see the shingles on their house, and the leaves on the trees – it also lit up their small airstrip, the hangar, and the whole works! The light just lit up everything around it in a big circle like an upside-down ice cream cone shape of light.

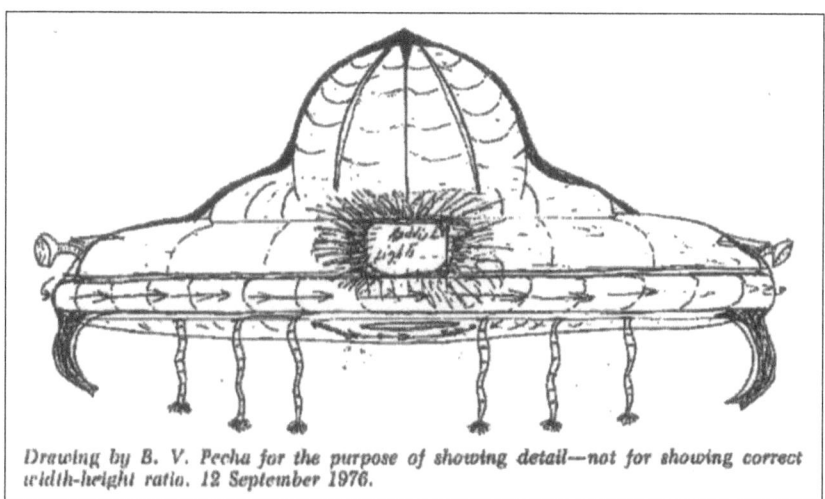

Drawing by B. V. Pecha for the purpose of showing detail—not for showing correct width-height ratio. 12 September 1976.

Billy Pecha's drawing of the craft. Credit: APRO.

As soon as the craft moved away a bit more, I ran into my house, down the hallway, knocking tables and chairs over, and hollering for Dede, my wife. I was trying to tell her to get the kids, and *let's get out of here,* but the only thing she could see was an orangey flash, which she thought was a meteorite at first. When the craft turned the bright light on, it changed the picture for her.

I was pretty shook up. I told her, "Get the kids and let's get out of here."

She got our daughter, Debbie, and I got Chris, my oldest boy. Dede made it to the pickup, and I moved down from the kitchen into the front room. Just as I started to open the door, the TV came back on. I went and shut it off. Then the refrigerator and the cooler came back on as well. I opened the door and we ran for the pickup.

When we got in the pickup, I put the backup lights on and panicked, *Oh Christ, these outrigger lights are starting to move again. It's going to see us!*

I had a blue pickup with a bright white camper on it. On a clear night, with the moon shining, that camper probably stuck out like a sore thumb. Dede kept pleading for me to turn the lights back on, but I wouldn't.

As we drove to town the craft was now coming across the land at about the same height it was over my house, about 50 feet up. As I got close to the cemetery, about another eighth of a mile down the road, it was over the cemetery and started back over towards me again. It now got over the top of us, and I told Dede, "My God, I think it's going to zap us." I figured it was now going to do the same with the bright light over us as it did over Slim's house.

However, all the craft did was cut across our path. I crossed over the railroad tracks and made a very sharp turn towards town and drove right to people we knew, the Arants. We ran to their door and started beating on the door. My friend came to the door, opened it and shouted, "My God, what was that?"

They had been up because the power had gone off, and they thought that they had the same problem that I did, that the juice had run out or something. I didn't even have to tell her; she'd seen it herself.

By that time, the main craft had a row of lights around it. It was making a high-pitched whine and heading rapidly toward the Sacramento area. All of a sudden, this thing shot off at a 45-degree angle at lightning speed and just completely disappeared. The other two craft, which had been hovering over the power lines, split in an instant in the same direction as the main craft.

Now the shock wore off. I felt cold, and I started shaking and mumbling uncontrollably in fear.

Around 1:30 AM, I called the Davises from the Arants' house because I was worried that the light from the craft that shone down on their house might have harmed them. I told them this was not a crank call. "What I am about to tell you, I'll finish tomorrow, but I've got to tell you now what is going on. Some strange things happened tonight."

I told them what I had seen and asked them if they were okay. Amazingly, it didn't seem to bother the wife at all. She said her husband was a pilot and they talked and read about flying saucers. She said, "We'd really liked to have seen them. We just woke because it was extremely hot in the house."

They hadn't a clue what was going on!

The next day I thought, *I'm still not satisfied; I've got to call the sheriff's department to make sure that somebody else saw this too, and it won't be just me starting something.*

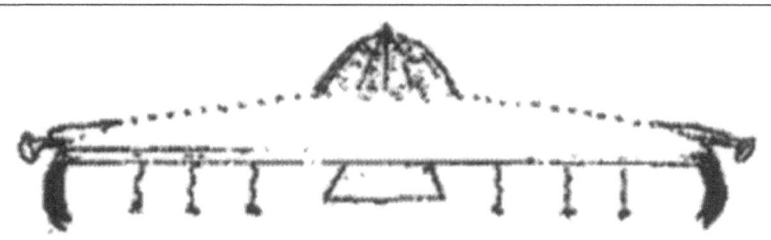

Side view of craft according to Billy Pecha's description. Credit: APRO.

I already knew what I had seen, but I didn't want to start calling people recklessly.

The sheriff's office told me, "We've already been contacted. There have been a few sightings right here. A few people have witnessed it."

I learned later that there were about eight witnesses in the town who saw the things, but a little bit farther away than we did. They included a sheriff's department lady and her son. We felt that one of the policemen also saw it, but he didn't want to make a public admission. He refused to talk about it.

Later we examined some of the foliage on our trees. A couple of the fruit trees began to bloom, in October, which was absolutely unusual; they don't normally do that.

The aftermath

Once the story got out, Coral Lorenzen, the co-founder of APRO (the Aerial Phenomena Research Organization, a major UFO research organization in the U.S. out of Arizona) contacted their director of research, Dr. James Harder, a professor of civil engineering at the University of California at Berkeley, who, in turn, called me and said, "I'd like to come up and see you on Sunday." My UFO sighting was apparently an extraordinary case, which they wanted to investigate right away.

I had repeating nightmares. The dream always started where I first saw the craft and ended when they all disappeared. I am looking out the window, going out of the house, and so on, repeating the experience, the same thing over and over. I can even feel the cool breeze. The sensation of the shock is gone.

It was suggested to me that I undergo hypnosis to recover more details, but I said no. I didn't think I should have to do that when there were other witnesses. I wasn't comfortable with it and I didn't know any of those people who wanted to do that. I was also afraid that something would come out besides what I saw, such as seeing saucers in the past. I didn't want to go there.

I didn't think I was taken up into the ship. There was no missing time. After we went to town and came back, we saw that our clocks were about nine minutes off. The power failure in the area was only about nine minutes long, which accounted for the time the power failed and the time it took me to walk outside and then the juice to come back on.

I was laughed at. The experience interfered with my life a lot but didn't change it much, except my belief. I never used to believe in saucers and figured they were TV sci-fi stuff – these things didn't actually happen. After this experience, I wanted to see one again, real bad, but not like I saw it that night, but from a distance, maybe even see it land. No doubt it would still shake me up a bit.

If I hear people today tell me their stories, I'm really interested, because I believe that they've seen something, too.

I don't know where they come from. The U.S. Air Force can't possibly have something that good. They might have something pretty fantastic, but they're not going to look ugly like the ones I saw. They're going to look streamlined with fancy stars and stripes and numbers of some kind on it. These had no writing or markings on them.

Commentary

The extraordinary Colusa Case was investigated in depth by APRO, and MUFON (Mutual UFO Network) also conducted its own independent investigation. In its detailed report, the APRO investigators said they found "no evidence that UFOs in the Colusa area caused the blackout or that the cause was located anywhere in northern California." Colusa, a farming community, is located on the west bank of the Sacramento River about 65 miles northwest of Sacramento. At the time, Colusa had a population of about 4000 people.

The official reason for the blackout was given as a disturbance at a substation in Victorville, about 60 miles northeast of Los Angeles and about 400 miles away from Colusa. Officials said the outage lasted about seven minutes.

More likely, the presence of the unknown craft did cause a power failure in the Colusa area. It is understandable that utility officials would not want to acknowledge that craft of unknown origin had the ability to interfere in the power grid.

Power failures and disruptions are reported in numerous sightings and encounters with UFOs. Appliances, computers, televisions, radios and so on malfunction. Vehicles "die." When the craft leave the area, power is restored.

The APRO investigators interviewed other witnesses, including local law enforcement personnel and the publisher of the Colusa Sun-Herald newspaper, who vouched for the credibility of Pecha. The investigators concluded that it was unlikely a hoax or prank, or could be attributed to the presence of normal aircraft or helicopters.

There have been other instances in the history of UFO research where beams of light extending down from craft appear chopped off. There is no explanation for this phenomenon.

CHOSEN TO WITNESS
Norma Jean Conroy

*Did a UFO reveal itself to a flight attendant and her husband –
and no one else?*

At the time of my sighting in 1979, I was a stewardess for United Airlines and I was also vice president of a development company. On a Sunday afternoon, we attended a barbecue at a friend's house in Hawaii Kai, a suburb of Honolulu. Around 10:30 PM we left for home; Richard Conroy, my husband, and I were driving separate cars.

We wound through the Kalama Valley neighborhood towards the ocean on the Windward side of the island. I saw some lights coming from off the Makapuu ocean area towards me. I was up around Koko Head, an extinct volcano and landmark that is the start of the Windward side of the island. There, the road skirts Koko Head and the nearby Koko Head Stables. The Stables was on our right, and the golf course was on our left. I didn't look at my watch, but I estimated later that it was about 10:46 PM.

I thought, *Gee, I wonder what airplane at this time would be coming over there, and they don't fly over houses like that. All the outer island flights don't run this late at night.*

I just kept looking at it, and then I thought, *I'm going to pull over and take a look at this.* I was really curious as to what it was, so I pulled over and my husband pulled over, too, probably thinking I was having car trouble.

I leaned over the steering wheel, looking up at this object. It was an unbelievable sight. It was beautiful really, when I think about it. It was so big, and I was in such awe of looking at this huge thing going over us. I just kept watching it. It wasn't moving very fast.

Richard came up to the car window, and I said, "Do you see that up there? What do you think it is?"

Richard said, "My God, what is that? It's huge. It's, you know… what are all those lights?"

I got out of my car and we just stood there with our mouths open. I kept saying, "Is that an airplane?" I just kept saying it, but I knew it was not a plane. We were not afraid.

Then the object came over the housing area, going really, really slow. It was all lit up, and as it was coming towards us, we could clearly see two large "headlights." The headlights were pointed in our direction, as it appeared to be coming right towards us.

I thought maybe it could be a helicopter, but because it was still far enough away from us that we couldn't tell at all what it was. Either it wasn't moving at all or it was going very slowly.

Sandy Beach and the ocean were on our right, and the mountains were on our left. It passed us on the mountain side. I'd say it was a couple thousand feet up, but it was hard to tell.

It was low enough to see that it wasn't an airplane at all, and that it had a whole bunch of blinking lights on its undercarriage, besides the two white "headlights." When it went over us, we could see underneath and it was just all kinds of lights, more than a dozen, 20 maybe. They all blinked at different times. There were red ones and green ones, and off-white ones, almost a glow color. The "headlights" did not blink.

We could now determine that it was shaped like a triangle from the front, and on the points of the triangle there were two bright lights like the front ones. You could tell it was a solid mass. There weren't any wings, like an airplane has wings that come out.

For comparison's sake, I held my thumb up in the air and looked at my thumb to gauge how big it was in conjunction with that. It was easily at least an immense two hands if not more, maybe three, from what we could see, as close as we could see it. It really was *that* big, and it was low, and it was going so slow; it looked like it was going to drop right out of the sky. It just was that amazing!

It was going way slower than a big airplane does when it lands. Planes aren't allowed to go over the housing areas that slow. That was super close to the housing and about 2,000 feet up. It was slow enough that I probably could have driven fast enough to keep up with it.

What I saw of the back of it was squared off. It flashed on me that, *Wow, the back of that is just completely squared off. I wonder what it is?*

It did make a sound that was hum-like, but it wasn't a hum of like a jet plane hum. More of a subdued roar. Any airplane that I've ever seen that close up to me made a lot more noise than that. That's why I thought it was a helicopter at first. And then, when I didn't hear any typical helicopter-like noises, as it got closer to us, I decided against it being a helicopter. Then the noise became like a deep hum, not loud. It was very non-mechanical. A few times we heard a kind of rumble, a *phruummm*, like a jet plane way off in the distance.

The sound was not offensive, and I doubt the people in the houses below even noticed it. They probably would have thought that maybe it was just a passing car. But it definitely was coming from that object.

It didn't seem to take any notice of us – it did not do anything that could indicate that we were noticed. It just went right over us. Next, it did almost a 180-degree turn. It was going away and then it came back! I said, "Hey there it is again." But this time it wasn't just going straight; it was going faster, and it was going sort of up and down. It wasn't just a straight smooth path like before. I said, "Hey, look it's moving funny."

Finally, it headed out towards the ocean in the direction of the island of Molokai, and disappeared in the clouds. It was going pretty fast by then.

We must have watched it for at least five minutes. Cars went by us. We were standing out in the road, looking up, and cars were just going by us. Evidently no one else saw it or noticed it.

After it was gone, we got in our cars and decided, "Hey, let's go home." When we got home, we looked at each other and said, "Hey, did we really see that?"

I was still thinking about it by the time I went to bed. I had a dream about a very large UFO and about 15 or 20 smaller ones, all different shapes, that were flying around, and people were seeing them. I wanted to say, *See, we did see it, because that's the big one that we saw, and now it's got other things there, too.*

Later I called the newspaper to see if somebody else happened to see it, but there were no reports.

We called a friend of ours, a pilot in the Air Force, and told him what we saw and heard. I don't know if he thought I was serious. He said, "Well, it doesn't sound like any airplane that I know of or have seen. And jet planes don't go that slow."

I didn't understand it. I kept going back to that it was something I had never seen before. I was kind of in shock. To me it was a UFO, pure and simple! It was not an airplane; it was nothing that the United States had as far as I know.

I think we were fortunate to have been able to see it. Maybe it *wanted* us to see it, whatever it was. Or maybe it didn't care at all if someone saw it. I don't think it cared, or it wouldn't have been showing itself.

I still think it's strange, though, that all those people that drove by us either didn't see it or didn't notice. For some reason, they didn't even look at it. It was almost right over us, and all they would have had to do was look up like us.

Maybe we were the ones who were meant to see it.

Commentary

One of the more perplexing mysteries of unexplained phenomena of all kinds, from ghosts to mystery creatures to aliens to UFOs, is, why does one person see them and another not? Two persons can stand side by side, and one can scream that "something" is right in front of them, and the other sees – nothing.

This disparity makes it easy for skeptics to dismiss the witness as suffering from an overactive imagination, delusions, or fantasy.

In the case of Norma and Richard, they both were witnesses, but were alone in that. If others in the houses below saw or heard anything, it was not reported, and may have been passed off as airplane lights and noise. The curious thing concerns those who drove by in cars and did not stop or look up. Surely some curious person would want to know why a man and a woman were standing in the road with their gaze riveted to the sky.

We can surmise that some people did not stop because of the hour, and perhaps location. Some passersby may have noticed Norma and Richard, but not been sufficiently curious to stop.

It is possible that Norma and Richard may have been "invisible" to others. Some experiencers feel that the encounter is meant just for them, that there is some intelligence behind it that selects them or zeroes in on them because of their interest. Norma and Richard did not notice any shifts in their environment, but some experiencers feel a palpable change in the "atmosphere." The air becomes very still, and other sounds go silent. Like Jayne P. in "The Hole in the Sky," they may even feel encased in some "bubble" of space and time, which dissipates when the experience stops. Abductees especially notice these shifts, usually prior to an abduction.

Norma and Richard may never know the answer why they saw what they did, and others did not. At the least, these kinds of experiences open the mind and convince individuals that the alien presence is real, and there is indeed other intelligent life in the cosmos.

THE HOLE IN THE SKY
Jayne S.

A rip in the sky vacuums in UFOs, witnessed by a woman driving in a UFO hotspot.

I see UFOs a lot. I don't know why. I've had a lot of paranormal experiences for my entire life, since I was a kid.

I make frequent driving trips up and down the Taconic Parkway along the Hudson River in New York State, because we have a second home upstate. I'm often by myself, as my husband travels on his own according to his work schedule.

The Taconic is a weird highway. There are a lot of stretches on it that feel creepy to me. People see a lot of UFOs while driving along the Taconic.

One afternoon I was heading upstate earlier in the afternoon than I usually go. This was in spring 2014, and it was a bright sunny day with barely a cloud in the sky. It was a Friday, a day when traffic is usually heavy on the Taconic, especially going upstate.

A hole in the sky sucks in UFOs at amazing speed. Credit: John Weaver.

I was driving along and suddenly noticed that I was alone on the road. There weren't even any cars coming in the opposite direction. *That's strange*, I thought to myself. I started to feel a bit uneasy – I felt that something was "off."

I kept driving along, trying the shake the feeling. Then I noticed that there were flashes of light in the sky. I glanced up through my windshield and saw some bright, shiny lights whizzing along, high up in the sky. They weren't acting like airplanes – they were moving way too fast.

I was near a spot where I could pull off, so I stopped the car and got out. Looking up, I saw the most amazing thing. It was like a jagged hole had opened in the sky, like part of the sky had been rolled back like those old-fashioned sardine tins that were opened with a key. Multiple ships – it seemed like dozens of them – were whipping at high speed into this opening. It was almost like they were being sucked in. They were silvery gray, and they glinted in reflected sunlight.

I watched in amazement. I then became aware of other cars driving by. No one seemed to notice what was going on except me – or if they did notice, they did not care or stop.

Suddenly all the ships were in, and the blue sky rolled back over the hole.

I wasn't sure what I had seen – a fleet of UFOs? Where were they going? Where did they come from?

Commentary

The Hudson River Valley in New York State is home to many unexplained phenomena. Even explorer Henry Hudson, who sailed his namesake river in the early 17th century, wrote of experiences with the "little people" that haunted the mountains and made a strange brew.

In the 1980s, the region was ground zero of a famous wave of black triangle UFO sightings. UFO sightings continue to the present, and are frequently reported up and down the river.

With her lifelong history of all kinds of paranormal experiences, Jayne may fit the profile of individuals who have a natural, extra sensitivity to alternate realities. She may have a more finely tuned "antenna" than others.

Her experience started with a shift in the environment, and a sudden isolation, as though she was caught up in a bubble of some sort. It shifted, however, when other cars showed up – even though no one else seemed to participate in her experience. Was she, like other witnesses and experiencers "chosen" to see this?

What was going on in the sky? Other witnesses have described holes that seem to open in the sky; things either come out or go in. "Things" include lights, craft, and even large and dark mysterious creatures, such as was observed at the famous "Skinwalker Ranch" in Utah. In one instance at the ranch, one of the occupants observed a hole in the sky and what seemed to be another reality on the other side.

The ranch has more than a 50-year history of unexplained phenomena, including UFOs, mutilated cattle, super-wolves immune to bullets, poltergeist activity, mysterious creatures, flying orbs and unusual magnetic activity. The activity was investigated by research scientists and documented in Hunt for the Skinwalker: Science Confronts the Unexplained at a Remote Ranch in Utah *(2005), by Colm A. Kelleher and George Knapp.*

A bizarre case involving a hole in the sky and missing time occurred in mid-winter 1988 in British Columbia. A man was finishing a house in a remote location near Littlefort. He worked out of a machine shop near the house and kept a record of his progress in a daily log book. On a Sunday, he went to town for food supplies, came back and packed them into the refrigerator. On Monday he was working along in the shop – and then suddenly he found himself standing in the house, confused as though he had come out of a fog. He had no recollection of going to the house, which felt strange, was neither hot nor cold, and was a bit dusty as though it had been empty for a long time.

He had no idea what day it was and found out from the radio it was Friday, 10:30 AM. Oddly, his log book was open to Friday – but all the pages between the previous Friday and that Friday were blank. Somehow four days had disappeared!

The food was untouched in the refrigerator. He was not hungry or thirsty, or dirty. He ascertained that his truck had not moved since Sunday. There were no footprints in the snow but his.

He did not know what to make of it and chalked it up to fatigue, and went on with his work.

Six months later, he had a dream in which he knew he was back on the Monday of "the event." A voice told him to walk down to a nearby lake. He did and looked up:

> There was a hole in the sky, somewhat like an enormous Saturn. It was as if I could see through to the stars... as if a portal. The "stars" were brilliant and dense. I was confused as to what I was seeing – not a solid object but a void. I stared. Then the thought came, *I'm seeing a UFO!* I was happy and excited. I had always wanted to see one!
>
> The millisecond I had the thought, an electric shock shot through me from my head to my toes and I was awake sitting up in my bed. This all happened at the same time. I immediately realized that I knew what happened the winter before. Oddly enough I had not even been dwelling on it much.

With four days of missing time, a hypnotic regression probably would have uncovered the details of an abduction. However, he let sleeping dogs lie. We do not know if he had any further episodes.

Jayne P. said of her Taconic experience that she had no missing time.

Do holes in the sky literally tear open? The hole may be the way the witness perceives something of an interdimensional nature. If UFOs come through interdimensional doorways or portals, it may involve a transition beyond human perception, which becomes "translated" into a way that human senses can comprehend.

UFOS IN THE ROAD
Various Authors

Do aliens use Earth roads and highways for landing points? Startled witnesses find something strange in the road in these two stories.

The East Bay UFO
Anonymous

A UFO makes a sudden and surprising stop above a normally busy, well-traveled urban freeway, which is strangely devoid of cars.

I had a surprising experience with a UFO when I was working in the San Francisco Bay Area. I had to come home on the freeway after working a swing shift one evening from four to midnight. By the time I was off work and got in the car and came across the bridge, it was around one in the morning.

I was driving across the Bay Bridge and was now on the East Bay side and about to make a turn to get on the Nimitz Freeway, Highway 880. Strangely, for a normally very busy highway, it was virtually empty, maybe a few cars, but certainly there was not the usual, normal flow of cars out on the freeway at just about any given hour, day or night.

All of a sudden, right ahead of me, a UFO was hovering above the middle of the highway. I stopped my car and stood by it to get a better look. It was egg-shaped and brightly colored. It had a glowing light, goldish but not actually gold. I certainly didn't want to drive under it.

I was very puzzled, thinking, *What is this? Is this some kind of a government thing?* I didn't really know. This was my first experience with a UFO, and I didn't know what to do. I just looked around, and nobody was around. It was strangely deserted. There simply were no other cars on the freeway that I could see. Here I was, stopped dead on the freeway. I got out of my car and looked up at this thing, and I didn't want to drive under it at all. I felt fear and panic and was very uncomfortable.

I got back into the car, and no way was I going to come out again for any reason. I kept looking up at it, and to my great relief it suddenly went straight up and then peeled off to the right and disappeared into the night sky.

I don't think anybody else saw it. However, after a few minutes, when I got a little bit further down the freeway towards Oakland, there were a lot of cops out on the freeway. I think they must have been aware of it as well.

UFO Hotspot in the Valley
Anita Sowles

A crazy, scary night in a UFO hotspot.

While I was in school in San Francisco, my brother Mike and his friend George would always camp in a hard-to-get-to remote area up Mill Creek Canyon in the Sierra Nevadas. You could only get there by four-wheel drive, but they had an old pickup that could handle this. You had to get permission to go into the land up there, it was so remote.

One evening they were camping and just relaxing. It was getting dark and they were by the campfire from which they could look down into the valley, which was known as a UFO hotspot. Many people have seen all kinds of things there.

That night, there were many unexplained, unknown lights in the valley – in fact, so many that the boys became frightened. As the evening progressed and they watched these lights maneuver in the valley below, they said, "We have got to get out of here."

So, in the middle of the night, they got in the old pickup and started down the hill. They got quite a ways down. But when they came around a curve, there was a glowing object in the road blocking their path. It was a reddish-orangish glowing object right in the road where they were going to have to go.

They were yelling to each other, "What'll it do, what'll it do?" They didn't know.

George, who was driving, flicked the lights on and off on the truck. The craft, in turn, shut its lights off.

They floored the gas pedal and cruised right past whatever it was and shot down the hill as fast as they could go.

Michael was very, very shook up about this.

Now among several of us in the family, we've all had our own UFO sightings. Not the same craft, of course, and not all the same sizes, but in that same general area. We talked to other people in the Mill Creek Canyon area, but no one would admit to anything to us for some unknown reason.

We don't know exactly what Mike and George encountered, except that they were sure it was extraterrestrial. What else could it be?

Commentary

Highway and road incidents with UFOs are reported from time to time. In some cases, the witnesses suddenly come upon one sitting in or alongside a road, or, a low-hovering craft forces them to stop their vehicle.

The most famous road UFO case of them all, the Betty and Barney Hill abduction, took place on September 20, 1961 in New Hampshire. En route home from a vacation at Niagara Falls, the Hills were driving late at night and noticed a mysterious light in the sky that seemed to be tracking them. On an isolated road, the light became a craft that descended low above their car, causing Barney to stop on the road. There ensued missing time. Under hypnosis, the Hills later recalled details of their abduction by aliens.

A few years later, at the onset of the famous Mothman wave in the mid-Ohio River Valley in November1966, another famous UFO road incident occurred. The Mothman wave was centered around Point Pleasant, West Virginia, from November 15, 1966 to December 15, 1967. Mothman was a tall, winged humanoid that made numerous appearances. In addition, there was a dramatic show of mystery lights in the sky, craft, Men In Black, poltergeist disturbances, high strangeness, and communications from alleged aliens.

One of the contactees was Woodrow "Woody" Derenberger, who worked as a sewing machine salesman in Marietta, Ohio. On November 2, 1966, he was driving home from work to his house in Mineral Wells, West Virginia, a route that took him along Interstate 77. At about 7:30 PM, he was on a lonely stretch near Parkersburg when a craft materialized from the sky and flew about six inches off the ground. It looked like a "kerosene lamp chimney," Woody said. It turned sideways across both lanes of the road in front of Derenberger, forcing him to stop on the side of the road.

A tall, slim, grinning, man-like entity in a dark suit emerged. He had a dark complexion and wore a topcoat over shiny blue trousers. He walked to Derenberger's car and conversed with him telepathically. He introduced himself as Indrid Cold, and explained that his people meant no harm. He asked Derenberger a lot of strange questions about the area, and then said he would be in further contact. He told Derenberger not to think of him as "alien."

Derenberger's encounters with Cold resumed two nights later, when the alien came to his home. When news got out, Derenberger was an instant celebrity, and people camped out at his home in hopes of catching sight of a "real" extraterrestrial. Cold told Derenberger that he was from a planet named Lanulos in the constellation Ganymede.

Derenberger said Cold took him aboard a spaceship numerous times to visit Lanulos and other stellar locations. Woody held court on his lawn to huge crowds who gathered to hear the stories. As Derenberger got deeper into his alien alternate reality, his earth life started to fall apart.

Skeptics derided Woody, pointing out that there is no constellation Ganymede. However, who is to say that Ganymede does not exist in an alternate reality or parallel universe?

Evidently Indrid Cold did the same thing to others. On the same night, November 2, two men also traveling by car on I-77 near Parkersburg stopped when an elongated object came down from the sky and landed in front of their vehicle. A grinning man emerged. He wore a black overcoat and kept his hands folded up into his armpits. He asked them some pointless questions about the area and then returned to his craft, which rose straight up and vanished. Evidently Indrid Cold preferred Woody for more interaction.

In 1975, a road incident with a UFO led to a period of high strangeness for a young Canadian man in the Bracebridge area of Ontario. On October 7 at around 8-8:30 PM, 27-year-old Robert Suffern got in his vehicle and drove down a gravel road to check out a mysterious orange glow spotted near his barn by his sister. Suddenly he came upon a large oval-shaped craft resting on, or close to, the road just 150 feet in front of his car. It was approximately 12-14 feet wide and 8-9 feet in height and was clam-like in shape. It had a crinkled surface and was the color of "the dull side of aluminum foil wrap," Suffern said. As soon as he saw it, it shot straight up at fast speed and disappeared. Suffern headed back to his farmhouse.

Moments later he spotted a creature alongside the road. It was about 4.5 feet tall with "very broad shoulders, which seemed to be out of proportion." It wore a one-piece, silver-colored suit with a white or light-colored "globe" on its head. The creature effortlessly vaulted over a fence and retreated into the pasture, moving like an agile ape.

After that came high strangeness: Suffern's television set blacked out briefly, and the orange glow returned to his property. His dog refused to come out of its doghouse for two days. He began receiving mystery calls in which he was told, "We have work to be done. Do not interfere." One call was from a male claiming to be "Lt. Colin Hunter" from the White House in Washington, DC, who was looking for information about the incident. He gave a return phone number, which Suffern called and was connected, a male military officer claiming to be Lt. Col. Waters. Nonsensical calls similar to this are reported in Men In Black cases.

It is interesting that in cases of highway UFO encounters, the witnesses report that the road they are on is unusually devoid of traffic, or *they are traveling through an isolated area. Missing time frequently occurs. Perhaps they have a time and space slip during the encounter – perhaps the time/spatial distortion is necessary for the encounter to occur.*

Considering these and other Trickster-style hijinks associated with close encounters, East Bay Anonymous and the young men in the Sierra Nevadas were fortunate.

GREAT BALLS OF FIRE
Colleen Hogan-Taylor

Fireballs in the sky are an unusual type of UFO, such as three witnessed by Oregon teenagers.

On a spring afternoon around 4 PM in Bend, Oregon, I was walking with two friends to my home near the west side of Pilot Butte. It was 1966. We were average 15-year-old, local, junior-high girls. Middle class, nice homes, no major worries, discussing our lives, sharing stories, laughing and plotting how to fill the pending hot summer months. Just three girls, walking home on a sunny day.

Suddenly in the northern bright blue sky, we saw three large fiery-looking balls. They weren't distant, like far away stars, but nor were they super close as in only a few miles. They shot across the sky and stopped. Yes, stopped! They were in a vertical line, appearing to be equidistant apart. Big orange-red, burning fireballs.

We were stunned... shocked. I ran and yelled to my mom who came outside to view this celestial craziness with us. We watched them for only a few moments – perhaps a minute or two – and then they shot off across the sky and were gone. Disappeared.

We stood there in shocked silence, looking at each other, our expressions conveying questions and wanting urgent answers. *Did we really see that?* We all nodded, *Yes. What was that? Is it coming back? Where did it come from? Where did it go? What could possibly do that?* Then, confirmation. We agreed. We had all just witnessed UFOs.

Bend's clear night skies attract astronomers, from professionals to the simply curious. The Pine Mountain Observatory is located just 26 miles outside of Bend, housed at 6500 feet. The local newspaper, *The Bend Bulletin*, used to print reports from the observatory about night sky objects spinning about the universe: planets, stars, comets and rockets. We'd seen those. We'd seen shooting stars and the Milky Way. But the speeding fireballs were nothing like those. This was no comet. There was no head or long tail. It was nothing like anything I had ever seen.

A few days later, there was a short story in the newspaper. Observers in other Western and Midwestern states also saw the same fiery objects racing across the sky. No explanation was given. There were no comments from the military or weather reporters of new equipment being tested. Only three strange, red fireballs shooting across the sky at rapid speed and then abruptly disappearing.

I look at the night sky and wonder all the usual questions. Are we alone in this vast universe? Are we visited? If so, by whom and how did they get here? I still remember that quiet, spring day in Bend, so long ago. I've only witnessed those strange objects once, but the memory and mystery stay with me. The questions still unanswered.

Finally, we three girls were not on drugs, were not prone to super fanciful imaginations. None of what I/we saw was made up. It was indeed, exactly as I saw and remember it.

Commentary

If the girls had seen a single fireball, the most logical explanation would have been a bolide, a bright, fiery meteor that streaks across the sky, often crackling as it goes. Bolides are large meteors that make a spectacular display, and sometimes survive the fall to earth rather than burning up in the atmosphere. These three lights moved in unison and suddenly stopped, however, which a meteor plunging to the earth would not do.

Fireball UFOs have been documented in America for more than half a century, and thousands of sightings have been reported. They were first reported in the American Southwest in the years following World War II. Green in color, they were seen around nuclear facilities like Los Alamos National Laboratory and Sandia Base (now the Sandia National Laboratory). They could speed faster than any military aircraft.

A secret military research effort, Project Twinkle, was launched in 1948 to investigate this phenomenon. Project Twinkle ended in 1951.

The final report issued in November 1951 stated:

> The gist of the findings is essentially negative. The period of observations covers a little over a year. Some unusual phenomena were observed during that period, most of them can be attributed to such man-made objects as airplanes, balloons, rockets, etc. Others can be attributed to natural phenomena such as flying birds, small clouds, and meteorites. There has been no indication that even the somewhat strange observations often called "Green Fireballs" are anything but natural phenomena.

The report recommended no further money be spent.

From 1951-1990, orange and red-orange fireball UFO reports averaged less than one dozen per year nationally. They then increased to several hundred a year from 1998-2010. Another spike occurred from 2010 to 2016, and then sightings decreased.

Data combined from reporting agencies such as NUFORC (National UFO Reporting Center) and MUFON (Mutual UFO Network) place fireball sightings from 2001-2015 at 11,066, or about 7.2 percent of all reported UFO sightings in America. They rank sixth in the most frequently reported shape. Witnesses report that the fireballs hover as well as speed through the sky, behavior that is not possible for bolide meteors.

Fireball UFOs remain one of the more puzzling facets of the UFO enigma.

BUZZED AT THE ZOO
Kenneth Synnott

A mystery light zooms in on animals in a zoo.

In the year 1993, I was employed by the Phoenix Zoo as a security officer. I had been on the job since 1985. One Wednesday evening, I was working the swing shift (4 PM to midnight), driving the security truck over the zoo grounds of 124 acres. I noticed an extremely bright light in the air directly above the lion and tiger exhibit. The light was oval, and so bright it hurt my eyes to look at it.

  I immediately called my partner on the radio. Before I could explain what I was looking at, he asked if I saw the light. At that point, the light was moving over my truck. I was approximately 100 yards from the lion and tiger exhibit.

  As the light passed over me, the truck's motor stopped, and the truck's lights went off. I sat motionless, more frightened than anything else. I could hear the animals from other exhibits making sounds that were very unusual for that time of night. All the indoor animals were in their night houses already, and couldn't possibly see anything.

As soon as the light passed over the truck, the lights and motor came back on. At times a bluish light shot down and immediately went off. The bright light eventually moved off the zoo grounds and proceeded west and stopped directly above the baseball stadium across from the zoo. After several minutes the light disappeared, and I could hear the sound of jets from the direction of Luke Air Force Base flying in the direction of where it had been.

It happened within about 15 minutes. My partner saw everything I saw from the front gate entrance of the zoo. We double-checked all the exhibits, and found all the animals had quieted down to their normal behavior. We called the head animal keeper and explained what had happened. The three of us agreed to keep the strange event to ourselves, and not to upset the other employees and the general public.

It wasn't many months later that a UFO flap occurred over the Phoenix area. I had heard of things like this happening, but never expected it to happen to me. I have visited Area 51, but I never saw a light as bright as the one I saw over the zoo.

Commentary

Animals react in a restless, negative way to the presence of alien lights, craft and beings. There have been cases of UFOs abducting animals, including farm animals. In the commentary of another story in this book, "The Grass-Eating Aliens," we noted that abductee Carl Higdon, who was out in Wyoming hunting when he was abducted, was taken aboard a craft where he saw a number of paralyzed elk.

No animals were missing from the Phoenix Zoo – perhaps the aliens were out on reconnaissance only.

Malfunctions of vehicles and equipment are common in UFO reports as well. Kenneth's truck motor mysteriously failed, and then just as mysteriously came back on when the UFO passed over and moved away.

Phoenix has seen a lot of UFO activity. On March 13, 1997, a mass UFO sighting in the skies over Phoenix, Arizona and Sonora, Mexico was witnessed by thousands of persons. The lights flew soundlessly in a

V formation and hovered in the air. One witness was Fife Symington, the governor at the time, who ridiculed the idea that the lights were of alien origin – although several years later he recanted and called them "otherworldly."

The official explanation was a military exercise involving the dropping of flares. Said one skeptic, "The Phoenix Lights were flares. Deal with it."

DANCING WITH ANGELS... OR NOT?
Angelica Chaparral

Plagued every night with odd moving lights in the sky, a young woman interprets them as dancing angels or fairies. Were they?

Let me tell you a spaceship story. For four years I was living in a cabin in a community in Mendocino in northern California. I was the caretaker of about 40 acres of land, including the gardens, the livestock, and the dwellings on the land. My cabin was way down in the woods; you had to walk a good half-mile to find me. It was on an unlit path with a lot of redwood trees and kind of down at the beginning of a canyon that had a creek at the bottom of it.

I spent a lot of time there by myself or with children coming in and out. Starting in the second year I was there, I spent a lot of time awake at night. I was also doing a lot of fasting and chanting at the time. I star gazed a lot, and began to notice stars that were moving around in all different directions – they were doing dances up there!

I was from an Air Force family, and never saw planes act like that. Then I thought maybe they were satellites. In fact, I thought of everything that I could possibly think of, but nothing made any sense. So, I decided that it was some angels dancing! I didn't really much care. One way or another, it was just fun to watch the patterns that they made.

For two or three years these patterns repeated. But there was one particular star that flashed like a bright light – it kept flashing brighter and brighter.

I thought, *Right. Somebody else ought to be seeing this!* I still maintained that it was just angels, because that was my way of thinking. I said to myself, *Oh, that's nice… dancing angels or fairies.* That was the reality I was comfortable with. I thought that I had this secret little cabin with a window into the magical world of angels and fairies, and I could watch them dance.

By the fourth year, I started noticing that whenever and wherever I slept, between two and three o'clock in the morning, I would wake up wide-awake and get up. I would look out the window, or walk outside, whether it was raining or cold, or even if I was stark naked, I'd just walk outside, look up at the stars, and there it would come – the bright light beaming through clouds, playing around and getting brighter and dimmer and brighter and dimmer.

And I would think, *Oh, isn't this interesting.*

But then I started to get scared, and decided it wasn't angels after all, and that it was probably a UFO. I don't know what changed that.

I started talking about it to people and they'd humor me along, saying, *"Oh isn't that interesting!"*

Well, no doubt, I did have a bit of an eccentric personality, and my community knew that, so they were now concerned for me. I started to really worry even more. I was telling people in the community, "Look, I know there are spaceships, and I know they're gonna come get me, you know. You've gotta do something."

Again, they'd just humor me saying, "Oh Angelica, you're gonna be all right now, and you know, things like that happen, but don't worry."

Right about that time the newspapers said that out in Pennsylvania there were these travelers called "The Two." They claimed they had gone on a voyage into space and came back, and they got a lot of publicity.

That was getting to me. I was thinking, God, now they're gonna get me, too. I didn't want to go anywhere. I was really feeling quite negative about it all. I began to think, *Well, I'm really losing my grip on reality.*

Finally, a couple of the community members said to me, "You ought to talk to a shrink."

I would go, "Man, I'm telling you there is nothing wrong with me; this is really going on."

They'd say, "Okay, you're gonna be all right, but just come out of your cabin more. Come into the community more. Don't stay down there so isolated."

One night, I woke up at three o'clock. I had three children who downstairs sleeping in the bunks, and I was upstairs with my daughter, Vanessa. I woke up and went up to the long French window. I opened it, and a light was coming towards me, and it was getting brighter and brighter. I just froze and stood there. *God what are they doing now?* It looked like it landed behind the cabin in the redwoods. I thought, *Oh, I'm not sure if they even know about me yet.* For some reason, I got tired of watching them. I didn't see them take off, but I saw that the light was there and very bright for a long time. Then I apparently fell asleep while they were still out there.

The next day, I went into the community and I told everybody, "These spaceships are coming to my house now. What if they come and get me?"

At that point, a couple of people said, "Okay, that's it… We're finding you another place to live. You need to come out of there as soon as possible. You need to go live in another commune, somewhere else. But you need to leave here right away."

I said, "Maybe you're right!"

The very next night, I looked up and there they were yet again! It was the same usual bright pulsating white light coming in at an angle. It was getting brighter and brighter and pulsating, and the whole room was flooded with this pulsating light.

I was both exhilarated and terrified at the same time. Everything was illuminated. I was terrified, because they didn't stop in the woods behind the cabin, but came right up to the window this time. And right in front it went *bzzzz bzzzz*. It was just like the frequency of my whole being was being magnified by the brightest light I had ever seen, right in front of my eyes – all I saw was like the sun right in front of my eyes.

I just stood there a while, and suddenly I jumped into my bed and pulled my covers over my head. I recited, *Our Father who art in heaven… Get this the hell out of here. What is this? Get this thing out of here.*

Then, my daughter, cried out, "Mom, Mom, what is it? What is it?"

I don't know exactly what she saw, but it certainly and finally was vindication! Someone else besides me saw this!

I told her, "Just go to sleep; it's nothing."

I couldn't take my pillow off of my head; I just kept praying over and over. I thought, *I can't handle it, I'm not ready for it, I'm terrified. Get it out of here; get it out of here; get it out of here; get it out of here; get it out of here; get if out of here; get it out of here…* until I finally fell asleep.

It was gone by the time I was awake.

I moved out right after that. I told the community, but nobody believed me. I mean, they wanted to believe me, but they didn't know how to act. And you know, I was really panicked. I moved right after that into a city community.

Whatever it was, it terrified me for several years. Maybe aliens were trying to communicate with me, and I freaked out and begged them to go away.

It was a while before I could look at the sky again.

Commentary

The blurring between angels and extraterrestrials is a common one. Interpretations are subjective and personal, and one person's angel is another person's ET. In the 1950s and 1960s, people who were contacted by the "space brothers" type of alien described them as attractive humanoids, much like depictions of angels.

In 1952, famous contactee Orfeo Angelucci was driving along the bank of the Los Angeles River around midnight when a glowing disc forced him off the road. Out stepped two incredibly beautiful humanoids, a man and a woman, who were bathed in light, reminiscent of the haloes and holy light surrounding angels. Later, he rode with them in their craft, visiting paradisal planets ringing with the music of the spheres.

It all sounds rather Biblical, and indeed, the angelic visitors of the Bible have been reinterpreted as extraterrestrials.

Dancing With Angels... Or Not?

In January 1967, Betty Andreasson (later Betty Andreasson Luca) was in her kitchen when a reddish-orange light shone in the window. Looking out, she saw five small humanoid beings approaching the house in a hopping manner. They passed through solid matter. At first, she thought they had to be angels, an interpretation influenced by her conservative religious background; she had no knowledge of UFOs or extraterrestrials. She was taken aboard a craft and subjected to a physical examination, and then had a "painful and traumatic" religious experience.

As her abductions went on, she realized the beings were aliens, not angels. Her daughter Becky also became involved in the abductions.

Similarly, there is a blurring between fairies and extraterrestrials, well documented by Jacques Vallee in Passport to Magonia: From Folklore to Flying Saucers *(1969). In fact, one could take descriptions of encounters with angels, fairies and ETs, strip out those terms and substitute "beings," and many readers would be unable to correctly identify them.*

People interpret the unknown based on the context of their worldview, beliefs, and comfort zone. Something that initially is interpreted as angelic falls within a broad comfort zone, but ETs do not. Most people have been conditioned by the media to be fearful of aliens. When an experiencer realizes that an "angel" may be an alien, fear of the unknown sets in.

This blurring of boundaries was addressed by Carl G. Jung, who considered flying saucers a "modern myth," a psychic projection from the collective unconscious embodying modern technology instead of the gods of old. In his work Flying Saucers: A Modern Myth of Things Seen in the Skies *(1954) he said:*

> In the threatening situation of the world today, when people are beginning to see that everything is at stake, the projection-creating fantasy soars beyond the realm of earthly organizations and powers into the heavens, into interstellar space, where the rulers of human fate, the gods, once had their abode in the planets... Even people who would never have thought that a religious problem could be a serious matter that concerned them personally are beginning to ask themselves fundamental questions. Under these circumstances it would not be at

all surprising if those sections of the community who ask themselves nothing were visited by "visions," by a widespread myth seriously believed in by some and rejected as absurd by others.

Vallee makes a similar observation in Passport to Magonia:

We may very well be living in the early years of a new mythological movement, and may eventually give our technological age its Olympus, its fairyland, or its Walhalla [sic], whether we regard such a development as an asset or as a blow to our culture.

In Angelica's case the mystery of the light was never solved. Angel, fairy or alien, it became part of a twilight zone of uncertainty. Many of today's "UFO" and "extraterrestrial" experiencers find themselves in the same territory.

Angelica's isolation may have contributed to the intensity of her emotions and to her ultimate reaction of fear and paranoia. This may have been compounded by the lack of understanding from others in the community.

MACHU PICCHU MAGIC
Kristin and Jennifer Shotwell

Twin sisters experience a strange light at a famous mystical site.

Kristin: We were in Peru in 2004. We went with our mother, so it was a twin trip and a mom trip. We went to Machu Picchu, and were among a few people who stayed up on top of the hotel.

We had some odd experiences. One was when my sister Jennifer and I went to do some yoga and meditation in the ruins after sundown. We were alone, and we heard flute music coming from the hills. We couldn't quite figure it out. It was ethereal, and very, very cool. It was enchanting and eerie at the same time. There were few people at the ruins, so we felt privileged to be about the only ones hearing this music. It was a *calling* type of tune. It seemed to be coming from somewhere, but at the same time, from nowhere, like we were being called or summoned. It set the stage for what was to follow.

The UFO

Jennifer: While Kristen and my mom were asleep, I was looking up at the sky through the ceiling skylight and I saw this thing moving around in the sky. It was a light. I couldn't see exactly what it was, because it was so far away, over the mountains past the ruins. It started doing a pattern in the sky like I've never seen before. It would go up, and then it would go side to side. I could not think of anything that I knew of that could fly or move like that.

I went to the window of our room and watched this for about an hour. Then the light shined directly into our hotel room and onto my face, and cast a beam of light across our room. I had to wake mother and Kristen up. I said, "You guys *have got* to see this!"

We all sat in this beam of light, watching the light in the sky. I watched this *all* night – whatever it was.

As dawn came, the light finally came to be in one fixed position in the sky. It wasn't as bright, and it did start looking more like a star. But I saw it, and kept my eye fixed right on it. Even when we went to breakfast, I could still look right up to where it was, and it was still there! But now, it looked just like a star.

I was not doing drugs; I was not drinking; I was totally straight.

Kristin: I was a huge skeptic about UFOs before this. But, I will never forget what I saw, and I know what I saw. I did feel like "they" were letting me know in their own way that I was watching them, and they were watching us. I knew that from the beam of light, because it was so bright. It lit up the room, and it didn't light up anything else in the hotel.

I felt transfixed in some way, and it was an eerie feeling. I could not stop watching this thing. The light had a quality to it that was not like an ordinary flashlight ray. It was silvery – I get the chills talking about it. It felt different on my body than ordinary light, and I was a little scared at first, but then I thought it was just so freakin' cool! I told myself, *I'm not gonna be scared. I'm just gonna let them see me watching them.*

I watched it all night, standing in this little window. When the morning came, and I went to take a shower, there was a little window in the shower, as well. I still kept watching it, and I still felt connected with this thing, like it knew I was there watching. Even when we went to breakfast, there was the skylight on the ceiling there as well, and you could look up, and I saw that thing again.

It stopped moving. I knew it wasn't a star. And, I still felt like the thing was watching me, too, but I was not paranoid.

Jennifer: The room was really flooded with this silvery light, like Kristin described. It's funny, I don't remember any particular silvery quality to it until she mentioned it, but it was not like any kind of ordinary light. There's artificial light, and there's sunlight, and then there's moonlight. This was way more powerful than moonlight. But, it did have more of a moonlight quality to it. It was very beautiful, and definitely much more powerful.

I felt like it was a show, like they wanted our attention. I mean, not my family, specifically, but they were letting us know that they were there.

Commentary

Many sacred and mystical sites have marked levels of unexplained phenomena occurring around them on a continuing basis. Machu Picchu is no exception. The mountain citadel was built in the 15th century for an Incan emperor and was a city for about 750 people. It was used for only about 80 years and was then abandoned, probably due to the incursions of the Spanish Conquistadores – although the Spanish never actually found the city. Some of the ruins have been restored in present times.

Machu Picchu is nearly 8000 feet in altitude; mountain locations are often places where people frequently see mysterious lights in the sky.

Many tourists visit Machu Picchu on spiritual quests, and thus have the underlying expectation or hope that something unusual will take place, or that they will feel transformed by the energy of the site. Jennifer and Kristen had no expectations of UFOs, but they were open to having extraordinary experiences. It is difficult to gauge how unusual was the flute music. Pan flutes are common in Peru, and sound, especially in the mountains, can carry over quite a distance. Nonetheless, the mysterious music perhaps primed them for another kind of experience.

It is also difficult to assess the mystery light, which the sisters felt had an intelligence behind it. Was it from a craft and alien-related, or was it of a more mystical nature? Experiencers are often left wondering exactly how to interpret what they see. Whatever it was, a UFO explanation fit for the sisters, and made a believer out of one.

A HUGE RED AND WHITE TRIANGLE
Maurizio P.

Three family members witness a triangular formation of lights that act in an intelligent manner.

On March 26, 1994, in the city of Hull, Quebec (five minutes from Ottawa), around 9 PM, I was riding in a car driven by my sister. My mother was in the rear passenger seat. I saw a spot of white light in the sky. The sky was full of stars and no moon.

After a while I noticed that the white light was still there. I asked my sister to turn onto a side road so that we could look at the light.

When my sister stopped the car and turned off the ignition, it all started. The white light moved swiftly from above a far-away tree to a point right in front of us. The light now formed a huge triangle with red and white lights all around. At the three corners there were big white lights. In the middle of the triangle there were three red rectangles, and below the middle one, a red lozenge.

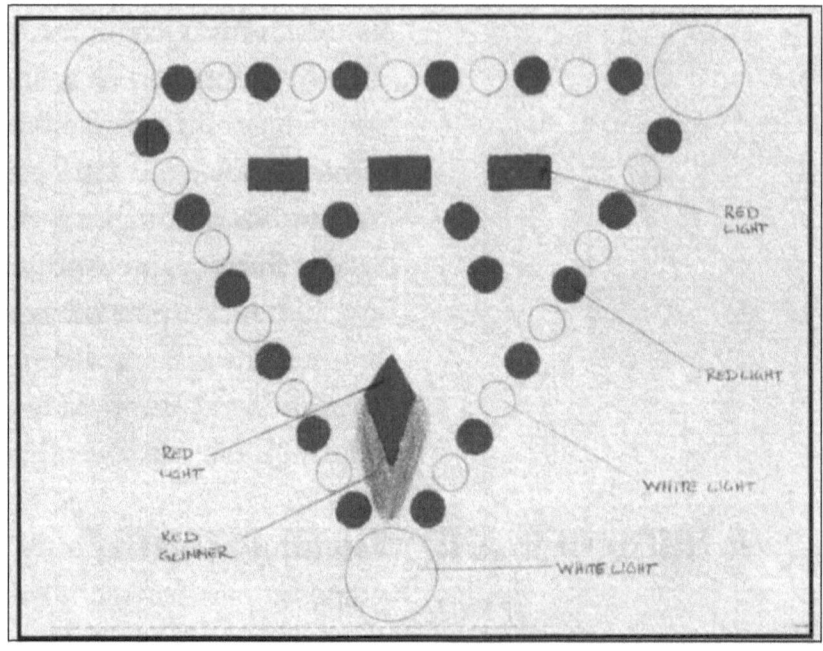

Eyewitness drawing of triangular craft. Credit: FATE Magazine.

I opened the car door and I put one foot out of the car, when I saw that thing moving.

I went back inside the car and the object flew off like an arrow.

We decided to go back home. That thing was going towards Ottawa.

Commentary

Many sightings of craft start out as mystery lights that are unusual: they are remarkably bright, oddly stationary, or exhibit unusual movements and maneuvers not characteristic of aircraft. If witnesses stare and become interested, a responsive intelligence is exhibited: the lights/craft move closer to the witnesses. Is the intelligence cruising around to see who will notice – or does it select someone to hone in on and get their attention?

In Maurizio's case, his retreat into the car perhaps saved them all from further engagement. However, there are cases in which no defensive action on the part of witnesses deters the intelligence behind the craft. It seems that if "they" want you, they will get you.

UFOs in triangular and boomerang formations are frequently reported. Sometimes the formations break apart and reform as the lights speed through the sky. Lights morph into craft, as this one did, taking on a triangular form with multiple lights in different shapes.

Triangular craft are frequently reported. One of the earliest cases on record dates to September 1952, when at least two triangular UFOs were seen during a NATO exercise called "Mainbrace." Naval personnel on board ships off the coast of Ireland observed a blue/green triangle flying over the sea at a speed of 1,500 miles per hour. Later in the same day, a triangular formation of lights emitting a "white light exhaust" was seen in the same vicinity.

In the 1980s, there were mass sightings of black triangular UFOs in countries around the world. One of the most famous waves occurred in the Hudson River Valley of New York State, where thousands of witnesses saw huge black triangular craft in the sky. In 1989-90, another mass wave hit Belgium.

UFOS OVER WASHINGTON, DC
George Wingfield

A noted UFO and crop circle researcher sees UFOs over the Washington Monument.

We had never visited Washington, DC, previously, and arrived at National Airport (now the Ronald Reagan Washington National Airport) on April 13, 1992 at 4:20 in the afternoon. My wife Gloria and I had flown from Raleigh/Durham, North Carolina, and were met by Susan Webster, who is also English, but who has lived near the city for many years. Although we had corresponded, neither of us had met Susan until that day. She drove us from the airport and pointed out many of the landmarks in the city. The weather was bright and sunny with hardly a cloud in the sky.

We stopped the car by the Tidal Basin of the Potomac River to wander in the sun and look at the cherry blossoms, which were at their finest. I suggested that we walk to the Washington Monument, which entailed crossing two busy roads, which we managed with difficulty. There were dozens of tourists there, mostly in a straggly line around the base waiting to ascend the inside of the great obelisk. Enquiry indicated that we would have to wait 45 minutes if we wished to go up in the elevator. I took several photos of the 555-foot-high monument with my Canon Autofocus camera.

Just as we were leaving the monument I said that I must get a photo of the White House from this vantage point and crossed to one side to do this. However, this photograph was never taken, for, as I walked, I glanced up again towards the apex of the great pillar. Over the top of the monument, travelling silently towards the west at great altitude was a bright disc.

As if this were not astonishing enough, there followed behind it a small fleet of seven lesser objects also shining brilliantly as they swept silently above the obelisk. Although there was no way of telling, these all appeared to be at a substantial altitude, say 30,000 feet or so. This estimate is based on comparison with jet aircraft at similar altitudes, but it was quite plain that these were not aircraft. The large disc-shaped object must have subtended an angle of about one-quarter the diameter of the full moon (7 minutes of arc).

Gloria and Susan immediately saw what I was pointing at and watched the objects moving silently above. I motioned to several people standing by the monument who also looked up, but most showed only limited interest or comprehension of what they were looking at. I found a boy with binoculars nearby and borrowed them to look at the leading object. Adjusting the focus with some difficulty, I was able to see that this object appeared translucent and circular.

By now the smaller objects had faded and only one or two remained in sight. Possibly their initial brightness was caused by reflection of sunlight from them in the position in which we had first spotted them. All of them had wheeled above us and were now receding again towards the east, in the direction of the Capitol. Soon only the large disc could be seen in the sky, dwindling in size as it flew away from us.

Then Gloria and Susan both saw a further small object, apparently much lower, flying rapidly westward. Before it went behind the monument it halted in flight, flew back again, reversed westward and brightened suddenly before apparently vanishing in thin air. This object I could not see despite looking along Gloria's outstretched arm in the direction indicated.

Earlier a boy had asked me what the first circular object in the sky was. "That," I said, "is a UFO." He looked somewhat puzzled.

I attempted two photographs with my Canon camera. One shows the Washington monument and the tiniest white dot imaginable, which may or may not be the disc. The other was not printed, and one can see that the negative shows nothing but blank sky.

By 6 PM, perhaps 15 minutes after the initial sighting, the largest object had faded to a minute dot and was eventually lost to sight.

We then headed back towards the Tidal Basin where the car was parked. Excited and bewildered by this totally unexpected sighting, we felt almost honored by this peculiar fly-past. Then a further object appeared flying roughly on a course from the Capitol towards the Pentagon, which was not visible from where we stood. This object seemed to drift silently across the sky, changing shape as it did so. At first it looked to be shaped like a cross, then perhaps a cigar, then like an airplane viewed from above. But this was clearly not an airplane and the only conceivable object which it resembled would have been an enormous irregular cluster of balloons strung together and tumbling across the sky.

If it was that, it would have been bizarre enough, but it was followed at a distance by a smaller object like those which had previously followed the disc. This object shone like the others but occasionally let out a bright flash, though it was impossible to say whether this was due to the sun catching a reflective surface.

In all we had seen 11 objects cross the sky, none of which behaved like any conventional flying object that one might have expected to see during the daytime. During all this time commercial jets had been flying in and out of National Airport though these were in a different part of the sky.

Although all three of us have travelled to many different parts of the world, none of us had ever seen anything like what we saw on that day previously. I have seen a few strange objects in the sky, most often at night, but have never been sufficiently sure that they were not something of a conventional origin to classify them as UFOs. On that Monday afternoon in Washington, DC, that was the only description that fit the bizarre objects that we had seen.

They seemed almost to be for us! Which is weird! UFOs were the last things we had on our minds. On countless occasions people have asked why, if UFOs exist, don't they just come down and land beside the White House? On April 13th it really looked for a time as if they would do just that.

Commentary

A Boeing 737 aircraft at 100 feet long with a 100-foot wingspan, or 10 to 11 minutes arc, technically is visible at 30,000 feet, depending on how the air bends and scatters light. George estimated the main mystery object at 7 minutes of arc, so some would dispute his contention that a disc was clearly visible – unless his estimate of the altitude was way off.

Regardless, George felt the sighting was a meaningful synchronicity, coming between meetings with various individuals with government connections who were interested in UFOs and remote viewing; some were rumored to be involved in hidden agendas. He had met a number of them in Atlanta, where he had attended a conference, and more meetings were to come in Washington, DC.

One of those meetings was a lunch in Arlington, Virginia that included three men from the CIA who said they were personally interested in UFOs and crop circles. George told them about his Washington Monument sighting, but, strangely, they did not seem to be curious about it.

During the 1990s, interest in crop circles skyrocketed, and many researchers literally took to the wheat fields to investigate the phenomenon. Theories abounded: they were made by earth spirits, extraterrestrials, or people. Mystery balls of lights were seen flying over wheat fields in England, where crop circles then appeared.

Ed Dames, a well-known remote viewer who had worked in the government's remote viewing program, and then formed a private remote viewing company called PSI TECH, had extensive conversations with George. He said his people had remote-viewed crop circles in England. What they saw were luminous spheres of light, about one-foot in diameter, moving slowly through the crop fields below the top of the crops. The crop then fell down behind the balls of light. They said that in some formations two or three of these balls of light actually worked with some kind of synchronicity.

The indications were that these balls of light were in some way controlled by extraterrestrials of some sort. At the time, George felt there was merit in this explanation – even though he and other key crop circle researchers were well aware of the people who were making formations. Did they account for all of them? The question remains unanswered.

As for the CIA: It is true that many crop circle researchers, especially those frequently in the public spotlight, "somehow" met or were introduced to the same government-connected individuals, who also were known to researchers in the UFO field.

At the least, there is undoubtedly an official interest in monitoring the activities of researchers who have the potential to sway public opinion about the alien presence on Earth. Both the crop circle and UFO fields have always been rife with conspiracy theories, accusations of disinformation campaigns, and high levels of suspicion about everybody.

A SKY SHOW IN KENTUCKY
Monte Val Stuart

A colorful sighting of multiple UFOs mesmerizes three witnesses late at night on a Kentucky highway.

In April 1981, I was traveling with two bowling buddies, Wayne and Jim. We had just completed a major bowling tournament in Memphis, Tennessee. We left Memphis on a Sunday evening at 8:15 PM and were headed for a second bowling tournament in Cincinnati, Ohio on Monday morning.

I was riding in the passenger seat of a Dodge van at the time we left Louisville, Kentucky on this long overnight trip. The third driver, Jim, was asleep in the back of the van.

I was leaning on my elbows on the van's dashboard enjoying the gorgeous moonless sky. Among the millions of bright stars, I noticed an object at about a 45-degree angle in the sky, about two-thirds the way up the windshield. I assumed it to be Venus because of its size, but could not understand why it did not have the normal brightness of Venus. It looked like an old, dull bluish-white fluorescent light. As I continued to enjoy the beautiful nighttime view, I kept returning to view the dullish Venus and wondering what made it appear that way.

After a while, still observing the object, I noticed it began to slowly move a short distance from its original position toward the lower right corner of the windshield, and stop. At that point, we had passed a sign on the right side of the road indicating a military installation to the south, so now I thought this was some type of military helicopter on a nighttime training mission. As I continued watching it, it moved to the right, horizontally and slowly, approximately three times the distance it moved before, and stopped again.

A short time after it stopped the second time, I was shocked to see a brilliant small red-orange object shoot out of, or from behind, the object and instantly stop.

Suddenly I thought I was now observing UFO activity. I looked at my watch and it was 2:55 AM. I estimated we had been on Interstate 71 for about 20 to 30 minutes. From the time I had started observing the object and now the second object, I hadn't said a word to Wayne, the driver, my bowling buddy, because I figured the objects would disappear, and I would be a laughingstock.

Approximately a minute later, a small brilliant maroon-colored object shot out of the original object, or came from behind it, and instantly stopped. Now there were three objects in the shape of an isosceles triangle that I was observing in the sky. About a minute later, I saw the brilliant red-orange object streak to the north horizon and disappear in an instant. The speed was unbelievable.

I looked at the original dull bluish object and the brilliant maroon-colored object. A few seconds later, the maroon-colored object shot to the south in an instant, leaving a brilliant maroon streak in its wake. After a few more seconds, the original object blinked out and I did not see it again.

I still did not speak a single word to Wayne. I continued watching the beautiful sky but at the same time paid attention to the horizon where the red-orange object disappeared. I could not see the south horizon because of the close proximity of woods and hills, and it was behind us.

After a couple of minutes, I noticed flashing white lights in the distance at the point where the red-orange object disappeared. My impression was that they were tower warning lights for aircraft. After a minute or so, I noticed the lights were flashing in a perfect circle on the horizon. I ascertained that this circle of lights was becoming larger as if it were moving toward us.

At this point I spoke to Wayne. I pointed in the direction of the circle of lights and asked, "Do you see anything unusual there?"

At first, he didn't see them, so I moved over, placed my arm on his right shoulder and pointed directly toward the lights. To my utter amazement, if not shock, he said, "I think we're seeing a UFO!"

As we continued along Interstate 71, we could now determine that the circle of yellowish white lights was rotating in a clockwise direction and flashing in sequence like a theater marquee. The circle was obviously getting bigger as it was getting closer to us.

I woke up our third passenger, Jim, and said, "You have to see this!" He had been sound asleep and was reluctant to wake up.

After a while, it was evident that the circle of lights was going to pass behind us, so I tried to convince Wayne to slow down, but for some reason, he would not.

After Jim woke up, the three of us decided to take the next exit so we could get a better view from outside the van. The exit at first looked promising because the ramp rose but then, unfortunately, it dipped into a valley and we lost sight of the object. We stopped at an intersection and got out of the van. Directly across the street was a brightly lit convenience store and from that position we couldn't see anything. We got back into the van and took the entrance ramp back onto the highway.

Back on the highway, we were amazed at how close this circle of lights appeared to be to us. It was obvious to me that they were going to pass behind us, but I still could not get Wayne to slow down. I went to the back of the van with Jim and we struggled to see structure or anything that the lights were connected to, but could see none.

Now, the vertical circle of lights disappeared behind a mountain. When it reappeared in a matter of seconds, it was no longer vertical, but horizontal. We could only see the lights flashing sequentially in a horizontal line from left to right. Again, I struggled to see anything that these lights were connected to, and I could not.

I estimated the circle of lights passed approximately one-quarter mile behind the van. Due to the topography of the area and width of the highway, I believe the formation was 400 to 600 feet in diameter and about 200 feet off the ground.

The lights passed behind a hill and we never saw them again.

We continued to our destination. I said to Wayne and Jim, "I've seen the first UFO activity in my life."

Even now, I remember it like it happened yesterday. To me, it is obvious UFOs are real.

Commentary

The duration of this sighting is unusual. Most sightings last anywhere from seconds to a few minutes. There are cases on record, such as the Betty and Barney Hill abduction case of 1965, where a mystery light or lights seems to track a vehicle for a period of time.

And, there are other cases on record in which once the light is observed by a witness, an intelligent response occurs, and the light then moves closer to the witness and/or tracks it. The light or lights may exhibit unusual aerial maneuvers. In this case, the lights moved from perpendicular to horizontal, but we have no way of knowing if that meant a craft turned 90 degrees, or reorganized itself in some other fashion.

Monte does not say where on I-71 the sightings began and ended, or identify the military base that he thought was nearby. A cluster of installations are around the northern end of Louisville where I-71 extends into Ohio, but we do not know which one is the logical one, and how far away it was from the witnesses. The proximity of a military base is used as a skeptic's debunking argument that witnesses are observing military craft on nighttime maneuvers. However, the unusual behavior exhibited by these lights is characteristic of other unexplained sightings, and convinces many eye witnesses, such as Monte, that what they observed was in fact not of Earthly origin.

THE FUNNY LIGHTS OF GUATEMALA
Melo de Leon

A Guatemalan family witnesses a UFO that lands for an instant and then takes off, as a wave of UFO sightings begins.

This happened in the late 1980s. My family, including my grandfather, my uncles, my aunt, and my cousin, Pepe, were driving home from Esquipulas, Guatemala. Pepe, who was about five at the time, looked out the window and said, "Look at the funny lights, look at the funny lights!"

They all looked at the lights moving around. The lights came lower and they saw a craft, a saucer shape with lights all around it. It had a row of windows like you would see on an airplane that were all lit up. It was really big, about the size of half of a city block. It hovered in the air about 20 feet above the ground, for about 30 seconds.

They pulled over to look at it better, and right when it touched the ground they all got out of the car to look. They were only about 30 meters away from it. Then it just whizzed off! It had just landed for a split second on the ground, but it suddenly took off, flying right away.

Maybe everybody looking scared them off, and the UFO just got out of there.

The lights kept appearing in the sky, and the story was all over the newspapers. For some time after that, people were offering tours to see the "funny lights." About a year or two later, the lights stopped appearing.

Commentary

Around 1988-89, a UFO wave swept over parts of Guatemala and excited large numbers of people. Mystery lights were seen nightly around 8 PM, especially in an area north of the capital, Guatemala City. Hundreds of sightings were reported nearly every night. People flocked to viewing areas, lining the highways and bringing telescopes and binoculars in hopes of seeing UFOs. Some individuals even brought organs to play the five-note "signal" featured in the film Close Encounters of the Third Kind, *to lure ETs in for landings. Others brought their salsa music.*

Some witnesses speculated that aliens were searching for ancient Mayans.

Skeptics dismissed the lights as small aircraft operated by drug traffickers, who usually fly at night. However, many witnesses, like Melo's family, reported seeing huge saucer-shaped craft, larger than a jumbo jet and silent, as well as aerial lights that moved extremely fast and did bizarre maneuvers.

Like other UFO waves around the world, the Guatemalan one stopped as mysteriously and suddenly as it started.

A GREEN CIGAR AND A DARK SHADOW
Charles Thatcher

Father and son have independent UFO sightings.

The Father's UFO Sighting

It was around 1958 or 1959 in Muskegon, Michigan, which was a very small town on the west coast of Michigan and on the east side of Lake Michigan. It was an area of beautiful vistas in a lot of places. We lived close to Lake Michigan, where there were a lot of little parks with picnic tables where you could catch the afternoon sun and look out over the lake.

I was probably eight or nine years old, and my brother Tim was 18 months older than me, and my sister Roxie was 8 years older. We were all at home with Roxie looking after us for the day.

My father, mother and aunt and uncle were all out together and had driven somewhere and stopped to have a little picnic in a park.

As they were having their lunch, there were clouds in the sky. Someone noticed that there was one very odd-looking cloud – a vivid green, cigar-shaped-looking cloud. They were all looking at it and wondering what it was and if it was even a cloud. It was fairly large and close. But then it just suddenly took off, just like that. They said it just disappeared into the distance.

When they got home, they were excited and adamant that they had seen a UFO, a flying saucer. I don't think there was any publicity about this green cigar flying saucer, though there were other sightings around Michigan.

They continued in that belief and maybe in that truth. For many years I never heard them recant that even once. All four of them were adamant about it. Over the years we began to read about UFOs, and sightings became more common. Other people were seeing this type of thing as well.

While being open-minded people, my father and my uncle Jack would not so easily and normally be convinced of such things. My uncle was very worldly, having been in the Navy and having traveled all around the world on a Navy ship during World War II. My father had been a state representative in Michigan and a superintendent of public instruction. He wasn't the kind of guy to just come to some unwarranted conclusion about something. Yet they both felt very strongly that they had seen something extraordinary.

The Son's UFO Sighting

Several years later, in 1962 or 1963, I had my own sighting with my best friend, Brucie, and his father. We used to go out in car trips looking for flying saucers. A number of other people in our neighborhood and our community did that as well at the time.

Brucie's family lived a couple blocks away from us in a home right on the edge of the small Muskegon County Airport. It had a small tower, and flights went in and out on an irregular basis. Brucie's father owned the only restaurant at the airport. Back in those days airports weren't so highly secured as they are now. We could go into the tower and you could drive all around. Our school was right on the border of the airport and we'd even play right out on the runway until we were chased away!

One night, I was over at Brucie's house, and his dad said, "Let's go for a drive and we'll look for flying saucers."

It was dusk and probably early fall – the trees were starting to turn but they still had leaves on. We drove all over and around the airport. We went out along some of the country roads by the airport. They were little roads, more like paths than paved roads. Mr. D. knew them well, so he was willing to take his brand-new Thunderbird out there. Brucie was in the front seat with his dad and I was in the back.

We saw something very odd that we at first thought was maybe a plane coming in, but strangely, it didn't appear to be on the runway path. It was quite level. It was a dark shape with a pulsating kind of light at the back end, not flashing like a strobe light, but rather pulsating.

We saw it coming. Mr. D. stopped the car and we got out into a field and watched this go slowly right overhead. What was weird was there was no noise. That astounded us. It didn't land, either; it just kept going.

We couldn't see any other lights on it. It did not have the shape of an airplane. It was getting dark at that point, but we could make out a dark shadow-shaped kind of thing and this pulsing light coming out the back with absolutely no noise.

We told my parents and the rest of my family about it. Their reaction was accepting; they didn't pooh-pooh us about it. But my father, in his rationality, said, "Well, you were at the airport. It was probably an airplane."

We said, "Well, clearly there was no noise. Airplanes make noise."

At least he didn't just pooh-pooh it as some parents might have. He accepted our opinions of what we thought we saw. Perhaps his own experience made him more accepting.

No one else confirmed our sighting.

I'm a photographer and a filmmaker, and to this day, I have a vivid memory of it, a picture of this in my mind.

Commentary

Reports of clouds that mask UFOs – or are even shapes taken by UFO craft – have become increasingly common since the Thatcher family had their sighting in the late 1950s. Skeptics, of course, say the cloud formations are natural, such as the disc- and saucer-shaped lenticular clouds. There are numerous reports of cigar-shaped craft as well. One unusual characteristic of the Thatcher sighting was the vivid green color, associated with fireball UFOs but not usually associated with mystery craft.

The son's sighting years later, even though near an infrequently-used airport, raises some interesting speculations about expectation and family connections. The desire to see UFOs does not necessarily mean that mistaken interpretations are automatic. As researchers have discovered over the years, the sending out of intentions for craft to manifest has an astonishing rate of success.

It is not unusual for multiple members and generations of a family to have UFO and alien experiences. Is there some genetic predisposition to encounters that is inherited? Do aliens monitor entire families? Or is it simply a matter of family conditioning through discussion? Perhaps all are factors.

SIGHTINGS
Various Authors

The unexpected sighting of strange lights and craft amaze and "freak out" witnesses the world over in these four accounts.

UFOs in the Nebraska Night Sky
Steve Cosgrove

A bizarre pattern of moving lights in the sky has no explanation.

In 1969, when I was 19, a friend of mine and I decided to leave Minnesota for the winter and ski bum in the Rockies. Destination: Aspen.

We left Minnesota in November in my friend's 1967 Camaro convertible and made it to Omaha after the first night out. We had no place to stay, so we went to the student union at the University of Nebraska to scout out some lodging for the night. The university was a short way from the freeway. This was the 1960s, so it was common practice to stop by a large university, talk to students and see who might have some floor space. Within a short time, a guy who worked at the union gave us his address and told us he'd meet us there in a couple hours. We could sleep in the living room of the house he and his friends rented.

We arrived at the house early, and with time to kill, we decided to stretch our legs. We were walking and talking, making plans for the next day. It was a crystal-clear Midwest night, not a cloud in the sky, and lots of stars.

As we were walking, I became aware in my peripheral vision that some of the stars seemed to be moving. Moving very fast. My friend became aware as well at exactly the same time, and we looked up in the direction of the movement and stopped talking. We saw a formation of five very bright lights right above us, quite different from the twinkly stars, moving at incredible speed across the sky.

In an instant, the formation seemed to rearrange itself and instantly move in another direction without slowing. This continued. There was no pattern to the movement, yet it seemed purposeful, not erratic. It seemed to go from one place in the overhead sky to another. One peculiar characteristic was the speed at which the formation turned – an instantaneous change of direction without slowing.

Even though the lights seemed to change places when the movement shifted, it always rearranged into V-shaped, five-light pattern, like geese. We speechlessly watched this for a couple minutes. Then the pattern rearranged once more and headed in a straight line from the sky above us to the horizon at extremely high speed and disappeared.

We looked at each other and asked, almost simultaneously, "Did you see that?" We confirmed that we both saw exactly what I've just described. Then we looked back to the sky to see if there was anything else. There wasn't. It was just a clear Nebraska night sky.

We walked back to the car, silently digesting this, and then began a discussion of "what do you think that was?" As there was nothing we could think of within the scope of our knowledge of natural or man-made phenomena, we concluded that we had just witnessed UFOs.

The Haleakala Lights
Jerry Haile

Haleakala Crater on Maui is the scene of bright mystery lights in a star-studded sky.

I went to a party at the Silversword Inn in Kula, Maui. At about 4 AM, several of us decided to go up to the crater rim of Haleakala and catch the sunrise. Haleakala is huge, the main volcano crater on Maui in Hawaii, and it goes up 10,000 feet to the summit. It's a national park with a ranger station up there, and it is, no doubt, one of the natural wonders of the world. The sunrises from there are spectacular.

There were four of us in the car that I was driving. We stopped about halfway up the crater to just look up at the stars. It's real nice and cold out when you get up that high. The stars look like you can touch them, they are so crystal clear.

I was watching the skies, and all of a sudden, I saw six lights going in a weird formation, very erratically all over the sky. I thought, *It has got to be a plane or something like that.* They were doing geometric patterns in the sky. They appeared to be quite far off. They were brighter than stars and stood out.

They moved in unison like a bird's wing or an M. I had the feeling that they were intelligently guided.

I was so astounded that I asked one of my friends if he saw what I saw, and then the rest of the people there, "Hey did you see this?"

Everybody agreed that they saw this pattern of lights moving around. Then the lights all just disappeared. The display lasted about 15 to 20 seconds.

I just figured they were flying saucers or some kind of extraterrestrial craft. I knew from living in that area that a lot of other people at Haleakala Crater have had sightings of things that were unexplainable.

UFO Over Medford, Oregon
Robert Broberg

A man has a rare close-up sighting of a craft with lights and windows that is anything but a conventional airplane.

In October 2010, I was driving south on Route 99, between Phoenix and Talent, Oregon, when I noticed blinking white lights that I thought were on a large plane on approach to the Medford International Airport. I looked up and saw a large object or structure that definitely was not an airplane. I estimated that it was well over 100 feet wide with windows and blinking lights at extremities. It appeared to be stationary or moving very, very slowly. The estimated elevation of the craft was approximately 2,500-3,000 feet. I watched it in my rearview mirror moving slowly northward toward Medford.

Later I checked the Internet and local media but found no indication that anyone else saw it. I decided not to report it myself, as I didn't want any publicity, particularly when no one else saw or reported anything. The other eerie aspect of the experience was that it was so quiet – I didn't hear any sound, such from an airplane.

Strange Light Over the English Countryside
Richard New

A bright white light descends upon a couple sitting out in the countryside. Its presence and behavior could lead to no other conclusion than it was a UFO.

When I was about 19, I was about to head off to college and get a place of my own. One day, I met a chick from right out in the country. She said, "Why don't you come down and see me this evening?"

So, I arrived about midday and we spent the day just cruising around and having a swim in one of the many lakes which were nearby. We spent the late afternoon having tea with her mom and dad. In the evening, when we were heading for the train station, I said to her, "Why don't we go and get a bottle of wine?"

We got a bottle of cheap wine for only 75 pence, which was a bargain compared to what it costs nowadays. We then headed off for the beautiful, wild countryside of Chalfont and Latimer. We walked through the forest and then found a place to sit, and smoke and drink and get into the beautiful natural surroundings.

It was about 9:30 to 10:00 on a mid-July night. The atmosphere was very quiet and laid back. We could look down toward a little lake, and in the distance in a valley, see "the big house," which was none other than a secret Ministry of Defence house, where people came to learn nuclear technology and the sorts of things that were done on the quiet.

You could see that it was all lit up with yellow spotlights, covering just about every corner of the house – every window, and so on – so that there was no way anybody could possibly climb up and not be seen and shot down in 30 seconds!

We sat taking all this in. The place looked very, very freaky albeit sort of quaint in an odd kind of way. Looking across, we could see green pastures and a little lake, and other valleys. It was quiet… just the right place for us.

I supposed it all was going to my head, the vino, so we indulged in a fair bit of kissing and cuddling as well, and were just having a good time.

The next thing I knew, there was a bright white light about. My first thoughts were that it must be an airplane at that distance, maybe about five miles away.

Then suddenly, for some reason, the atmosphere changed. I was lying there, and I was really into the chick and she was into me, and we were just having a good time. In less than 10 seconds, this far-away light was now about 300 yards from us.

At first, we tried to explain it away naturally: it was an airplane or a jet. Then we thought it must be a satellite. But the white light came really fast and low down, and then it stayed where it was. Just a white, completely round, bright light. It did not light up the whole area, but we could see that for sure, it was no airplane, and it was no satellite, either. We could not see a solid object; it was a globe-shaped white light.

We continued to sit there and drink some more wine. We sat there at peace, not having any bad thoughts. Meanwhile, the light or whatever it was, stayed there.

Then it dawned on us that it could not be anything other than a UFO! Suddenly, we heard a rustle. Maybe it was just the wind, but it felt like as though something had moved in back of us. It really spooked us. We could not relax any more. The atmosphere went from quiet to an unnatural dead silence.

We became paranoid. As soon as we started to talk in a paranoid manner, the white light went from an arrow to a point, and quickly disappeared. It was like it picked up on our speech or paranoia, sensed our disquiet, and removed itself without a sound. It was gone before we could say "up."

It really frightened me because I thought, *Well, maybe they're just down here to keep an eye on the Ministry of Defence, and they became interested in what* WE *had to say!*

But since we showed paranoia, even for an instant, maybe they thought that we were in their way somehow. Who can say?

There was no way that it was a quiet jet or anything else, because it was stationary, and there are very few craft that can stay permanently in one place with a consistent light and no noise, and then disappear with a flick of the fingers. It had to be a UFO. There was no other conceivable explanation for it.

It was one of the most freaked-out experiences that I had ever had.

Commentary

Erratic lights in formation and moving at high speed, such as described by Steve Cosgrove in the first story, are perhaps the most commonly reported UFOs. Many people see craft, as Robert Broberg did in the second story. Most such experiences probably go unreported, and the witnesses are left just shaking their heads.

When such sightings are reported, they are usually dismissed as mistakes on the part of the witnesses, or natural aircraft. Robert Broberg's proximity to an airport would immediately raise the objection that he mistook a plane for a UFO. Similarly, the same objection could be levied against Richard New's account of his U.K. experience, because of his position on a hill looking at a distant light. "You just thought you saw..." is the usual dismissal.

When witnesses counter that the high speeds and aerial maneuvers, the descriptions of craft, and the intelligent response to their thoughts defy explanation, most authorities still do not take them seriously. UFO collection and investigation organizations have countless such reports.

UFO lights and craft are frequently reported at Haleakala; there have even been waves of sightings of lights and formations of lights that move together. Some witnesses also have reported missing time. Many of the reports come from persons who have traveled there in the pre-dawn hours to see the sunrise. The ancient Hawaiians called Haleakala the "Crater of the Sun."

ALIEN ENCOUNTERS

THE ROAD TRIP ABDUCTION
Judy Kendall

Three sisters experience a lengthy period of missing time on a road trip and realize later they were abducted by aliens.

Missing Time

I had taken a trip to my grandmother's in Bodega Bay, California with two of my sisters, and we were on our way back from Bodega Bay to my parents' house near Zamora. Normally, the trip probably would take 2-1/2 hours at the most, but we allowed about three hours for the trip.

On the way home there was a particular part of the road that crossed what is now called Interstate 505. There's a part of the road that narrows, where there's a flashing yellow light on a sign that reads, "Road Narrows." Then you go across this bridge, which goes over a creek.

We went across the bridge and headed for our turnoff to home. But for some reason, we weren't getting to our turnoff. We didn't know why, but we weren't getting there. We were getting tired, and we couldn't figure out what was happening.

At about the same time, one of my sisters and I both said, "Wonder why we are not getting to our turnoff?" About then, we found ourselves back again in front of that same flashing yellow light and sign, where they showed the road narrowed. We crossed the bridge for the second time! This time, we went directly to my parents' house.

We discovered that we had lost about 4-1/2 hours of time! We didn't know what happened. We had no idea.

My dad thought we were partying some place and that we made this entire story up. We insisted we did not. Finally, he got a map out and he checked it to make sure that we couldn't have gone around in a big circle somewhere, somehow, and merely wound up coming back on the road to the same place.

I told him he was ridiculous, because I knew the road. We'd been there, lived in the area all our lives, and there was just no way that we would have gone around in a circle. Besides, we were going on a straight road and I knew it.

He checked the map anyway, and saw there was no road that we could have taken that would have gone around in a circle to come back up on the road with the flashing yellow light.

Then we all forgot about it. We didn't talk about it anymore after that, other than the fact my mother had called my grandmother to check and see if we did leave at 5:30 PM, which in fact we did, and we got home sometime between midnight and 12:30.

Earlier UFO Sighting

A few years before, I had seen what I thought was a UFO out by Yolo, which was about 10 miles north of Woodland, where I had been visiting with friends. On my way back into town, around 11:30 at night, I saw what I thought was a UFO, because it was changing in color. It started out as a white light, really bright, and then it went way down to a deep orange color, and it was hovering right over power lines over a gravel pit.

I remember thinking when I first saw it, *Gee. They must have gotten new night-lights at the gravel pit.* It turned out that it wasn't night-lights at all, so I think it was a UFO. I'm pretty sure it was.

In fact, I would almost stake my life on it! While I watched it, the lights changed three different times. It went from a real bright white light down to the orange color, and did it three times. The third time, it just shot straight up and was gone. It was gone before you could even blink.

I got back into my apartment in town, and I called my girlfriend where I had just left and said, "You're not going to believe it, but I just saw a UFO."

She said, "Oh, I believe it." Then, interestingly, she said, "Did you and your sisters ever figure out what happened to you when you lost your 4-1/2 hours of time?"

I said, "No." I thought it was strange that she brought it up, but then figured it was because of her interest in UFOs. She'd been studying and reading, which I never had done. She knew a lot about them. Maybe she knew something about the time lapses and that sort of thing.

I said that this friend of mine from Bodega Bay had suggested that we had gone through what she called a "time warp." But I couldn't find out what a time warp actually was.

I then told her, "I've looked everywhere, and I can't figure what it is! I can't find it anywhere."

She said, "I'll tell you who can tell you. Why don't you write to J. Allen Hynek? He's a professor of astronomy at Northwestern University."

I said, "All right."

The UFO abduction

I wrote to Dr. Hynek, and I told him what had happened. I asked him what a time warp was. I also told him that we'd lost 4-1/2 hours of time, and that we'd gone across the bridge twice. "What do you think happened to us?" I asked.

He wrote back, saying that a "time warp" was a science fiction term and not a proper term to use. The proper term would be a "time lapse." However, Dr. Hynek didn't feel that that was what actually happened to us. Furthermore, he said that he would like to have some of his investigators come and talk to me.

Dr. Hynek arranged for Paul Cerny of Northern California MUFON (Mutual UFO Network), based in the San Francisco Bay Area, to come and talk to me.

First, Mr. Cerny talked to my boss, Joe. I guess he wanted to find out if I was a "flake" or whatever – that was the word he used.

I told him, "I could have told you that!"

My boss told him that I wasn't, of course. Thank goodness for that!

Next, he arranged to have a hypnotist come out and talk to me. He told me that they felt that possibly we had been abducted by a UFO. My heart went into my throat, and I thought, *Oh no, he's got to be kidding. No way!*

He said, "One way we can find out for sure is to put you under hypnosis and regress you and find out what happened at that time." He contacted a Dr. Alvin Lawson, from Long Beach, a professor of English at Cal State at Long Beach. A super nice guy. He talked to him, and he, in turn, got a hold of his friend, Dr. McCall, from down there as well. They both flew up to Woodland, near to where I was living.

They brought all sorts of people along with them to listen to the hypnosis session. Dr. McCall came along to do the hypnosis.

They all came to my apartment. Carol, my girlfriend, was there, and I had some other people there, too, to listen and to watch and make sure that everything was strictly on the up and up.

And it was. They were very professional about it, and they were very nice to me, and they treated me with respect. It wasn't a silly thing at all – they were very serious about what they were doing.

They regressed me, putting me under hypnosis. Then, through the hypnosis, they found out that our car was abducted right off the road and into a craft. Then we, in turn, were taken out of our car and put into separate rooms. My two sisters were not together in the same room. I could hear one of my sisters crying in another room and calling out my name. The other one – I had no idea where she was, at all. I never heard her or saw either one of them while we were on the craft. When they put us back in the car, then I saw them again.

I was taken into a room; I don't know all the details. There are parts missing, which I hope someday to go under hypnosis again and see if I can get some more detail. I ended up undressed on a stainless steel table with a sheet over the top of me. There were four *"people"* in the room.

I was lying on a table, and to my left was a lady who appeared to be human. I'm not sure of her height; I think she was somewhere between 5 feet 4 inches and 5 feet 6 inches tall. She was definitely human; I don't think there was any question about that. She had shoulder-length black hair, blue eyes and fair skin. She was of medium build. She wasn't heavy or fat.

The other three were standing at the end of the table. I would call them *"aliens."* They were in gray-colored suits that completely covered them, and they had big masks over their faces. The masks reminded me of pilots' masks from World War II movies. I could see their eyes, which were big and round. I don't really know the color; I would say probably orange or yellow, something like that. They weren't blue or brown like our eyes.

Over to my right, I saw coming in from a hallway what I call the "witch doctor." He was the one that frightened me so bad. I was so afraid that when I was under hypnosis – they brought me through it so many times – I finally had to say, "I don't want to see that guy anymore!"
I would not even talk to them until they let me go right on past that part of the hypnosis.

The witch doctor was very tall compared to the rest of them, maybe close to 7 feet tall, or at least somewhere between 6 and 7 feet. He had a very large head compared to the rest of his body; it was not in proportion. The top of his head was quite bulbous – over-exaggerated, you might say. This part of the head, the cranium, came down into like a jaw. I would say, the head looked a lot like a light bulb, but the top of the light bulb was more exaggerated, more bulbous looking.

He had eyes that covered the whole cavity, like what would be from our eyebrows clear down to our cheekbones. The eyes were grasshopper-like. That's the only thing I could relate to, as far as what they looked like. Insect-looking, I would say. And they were transparent-looking. Their pupils were red, and you could see red veins in them. His head was bald; there was no hair at all. No hair on his face, no hair on his head. His skin was transparent, very thin, and you could see through his skin that he had veins and arteries that looked like ours. But to look at ours, they're blue; to look at his, they were red.

He had gloves on and appeared to have five fingers on each hand. I would say that he had hands like we do, unless that was just to create a look. I don't really know.

The "witch doctor" alien terrorizes Judy. Credit: John Weaver.

I was not afraid until the witch doctor came in and walked towards me. I cried, and I was really just hysterical. The "human" girl, said, "It's okay, it's okay."

The other aliens didn't scare me. I was skeptical of them and I worried, but having the female human girl there, I wasn't quite as scared. It was like, if I really wanted to communicate with her I could, and I didn't feel threatened at all. But as soon as that big ugly guy came in, then I really got frightened.

The witch doctor spoke to me in English, but it sounded like he was talking through a megaphone, almost like a machine type thing. The girl on my left talked to me, too, and kept saying, "It's okay, Judy, it's okay."

I thought, *How did she know my name? I didn't tell her my name.* I couldn't understand why they knew my name.

Then I thought, *Well, shoot, if they knew how to pick me up off the ground or take my car off the ground, they certainly probably knew our names or knew a way of finding out.*

I was examined by, I don't know how many of these beings. The three that were standing at the end stayed there the whole time. They didn't do any examining, but somebody from behind me did. I don't know who it was; I didn't see them.

The witch doctor being appeared to be the superior one of all of them. They didn't communicate out loud with each other, but they'd look at each other, and just did what they wanted or what they were supposed to. It looked like they were talking to each other, but it was a telepathy type of talking. They did not ask me anything.

It was like I was a guinea pig. They just wanted to see what was going on with our bodies or something. I thought that it was maybe a purely scientific physical examination type of thing.

They treated me like I was... like we have the apes, we have mice and rats and such that we use for experiments. I felt like I was being used as an experiment or as a learning kind of thing. I felt like I was being treated as a lower level or lower class, or lower form of life than they were. It was like I was the dog and they were the master type of thing.

After they were through examining me, I was put back in the car. I was carried back to the car by four aliens, the ones in the suits with the masks, one on each arm, and one on each leg. They just kind of went *whoosh...* threw me right into the car, so perfectly. It was really funny; it was like they knew just exactly how hard. I landed exactly behind the steering wheel. I don't know how they judged it or how they did it, but they just threw me back into the car perfectly.

When I landed in the car, my two sisters were not there. I sat there for a long time waiting for them. I didn't know where they were. I sat there for a long time wondering where they were. I began to get worried.

Soon I just looked over and there they were. It was just as if they materialized out of thin air. I know the aliens didn't throw them in like they did me, and I didn't see them coming from anywhere, so I didn't know how they got in there, but they did get back in the car.

The next thing I knew we were back on the road in front of the flashing yellow light again, going across the bridge, and that was it.

Aftermath

I went under hypnosis. I want to go under hypnosis again to find out more information, but I'm not sure if I really, really do want to go under again, if I have to run into him – the witch doctor – again.

I don't know where they were from. I think that there are probably other planets besides Earth that have life, and there probably are people that are a lot more superior to us. We haven't been here that long, so it seems possible to me that there is life on other planets, and they are a lot more advanced than we are.

I did not attempt to ask them anything, which really surprised me, because I'm usually inquisitive. I couldn't understand why I didn't ask them anything, and why I didn't try to find out what they wanted, what they were doing, and where they were from. But I didn't even ask. While I was under hypnosis, I remember saying that. I didn't understand why I didn't ask them any questions.

I have mixed feelings about the experience. Sometimes I'm glad I went through it, and sometimes I'm not. I've met a lot of fantastic people through it. I've always believed that there are UFOs. I've never discredited anybody who has said they have been abducted. I'm definitely a believer now, and I really feel that it did happen, even though I did not see a craft. The more I think about it, the more I am sure that it was an actual physical thing.

I've had some people say, "Well, maybe it was just a psychic thing and that you were in a different level of consciousness, and maybe you just imagined it."

I always answer, "Well, I can't imagine losing 4-1/2 hours of time. My sisters both know that they lost the time, too, and that we went across the bridge twice." If we hadn't gone across the bridge twice, and if we hadn't come down twice in front of the sign, I guess I might have thought differently of it.

My sisters both talked about it in the same way, and it was just like maybe subconsciously we knew that we were up in space someplace, or wherever we were, and brought back, but we came down on that road. So, the way we've talked about it was certainly an indication that we had been up off of that road.

I don't know if I have had any contact with them since or that I will again. I've had weird feelings, funny feelings, thinking that there was "somebody" around, somebody watching me. I feel more jittery. However, we've also had a lot of crime happening in our town. For instance, a lady just down the street two blocks away, who is a good friend of our family's, was raped and beaten. So, I don't know if my feelings have something to do with worrying about whether somebody's going to come in my window, or if it's them. I've had the feeling before that happened to that woman, however.

My sisters don't want anything more to do with it. They are just scared to death. They agree that we went across the bridge twice; they agree that we lost the 4-1/2 hours of time, but they don't even want to think that it was even possible to be picked up by a UFO.

Commentary

The UFO literature is filled with abduction accounts in which the victims were terrified and psychologically scarred for a long time, perhaps for life. It is not unusual for abductees to avoid remembering their experiences.

The details of abductions are usually recovered under hypnosis, though some individuals have conscious memory recall. Like Judy and her sisters, the experiences often start with missing time. Other abductions start in the bedroom, and the sleeping victim is paralyzed and transported out.

There is often present a "head" alien who looks markedly different than the rest; some are described as praying mantises, and many have "insect-like" features, like the witch doctor. Others have been described as reptilians. Both insect and reptilian forms play upon some of the deepest and oldest innate fears of human beings.

Many abductees say they are treated like a lower life form, as though they are part of an experiment. They have no idea where they are and why they are there. Terror and pain are part of the experience.

Some abductees, however, say they have been treated kindly by aliens, and informed that they are needed for a hybrid breeding program.

How long have abductions been going on? In modern post World War II ufology, they have been reported from the 1950s, and have had a spotlight since about the 1980s. Abductions by other "alien" beings have been reported throughout history. The fairies were famous for their abductions, paralyzing and whisking people away while they slept. Evil fairies would carry people into the air and drop them to the ground.

Once again, the question arises, are the phenomena attributed to extraterrestrial beings a modern version of an ancient interplay between humans and unknown aliens, suited to our worldviews and technology?

POD BEINGS AT SILBURY HILL
Ron Russell

Alien "little people" driving pods of light make an appearance at the famed Silbury Hill in England, astonishing witnesses.

A young woman, Judy Young, came up to me at the Glastonbury, England crop circle and paranormal conference in August of 1994. She said, "I know you belong to MUFON and CSETI. I just don't know what to do. These young kids who knew my ex-husband came to me yesterday and told me an astonishing story of a UFO sighting they had on Silbury Hill. They never had anything like this happen to them before, and they don't know quite what to do with it."

She continued, "And when I told a few people, they kind of got skittish, and I don't know how to handle this."

I told her, "Well, I can talk to the kids and maybe give them some good advice, and, of course, I'd like to take their story down."

I had been working in the area for the previous week with CSETI and our Skywatch International team. CSETI stands for the "Center for the Study of Extra terrestrial Intelligence," and "MUFON" is the Mutual UFO Network, the largest UFO research group in America. Both groups are involved in the investigation of UFO phenomena. They just have different approaches to it. I was, of course, very interested to hear what these kids saw, since it may have related to the work we did, too.

I met Paul, Sonya and Rob. They were in their early twenties. A couple of them were musicians. They didn't do drugs. There didn't seem to be anything untoward about them. Sonya worked as a manager.

On a lark, on the 31st of July 1994, Paul, Sonya and Rob decided to drive to Silbury Hill and camp out for the night. They were joined by two other friends. They went up on the flat top of the hill and took a position facing the nearby West Kennet Long Barrow, an early Neolithic construction. The two friends did not stay long, and left to join a skywatch group elsewhere. There were also five teenagers on another edge of the hill, who were drinking and being noisy.

Paul, Sonya and Rob had a portable tape player with them and played a tape called, of all things, *"Abduction!"* And they played this tune, *"Implant!"* Not the kind of tune you'd want to be playing late at night!

Around 1 AM, the atmosphere abruptly changed. Dogs in the distance started barking and Sonya noticed a peculiar smell. There were whispering voices, and "something" ominous seemed to be coming up the hill. Then all went silent and still.

By 1:30 AM, they noticed that the valley below was filling with fog, which came up to near the top of the hill where they were. They shined their flashlights into it.

They saw off in the distance to their left, coming from the direction of Walden Hill towards Avebury, two little spheres of orange light about the size of tennis balls. They were moving in a bumpy way, like car headlights or bicycle lights. The lights were not moving on the ground, however, but through the air at about their level of the top of Silbury Hill, which is about 180 feet above the ground. They watched these lights thinking, *My gosh, what's this?*

The lights came across the A4, the old Roman road right in front of Silbury Hill, and then split into several lights in the shape of tetrahedrons about six feet long. They seemed to be craft. The tops of the two pods were glowing with orange light, and the sides were glowing with white light.

POD BEINGS AT SILBURY HILL

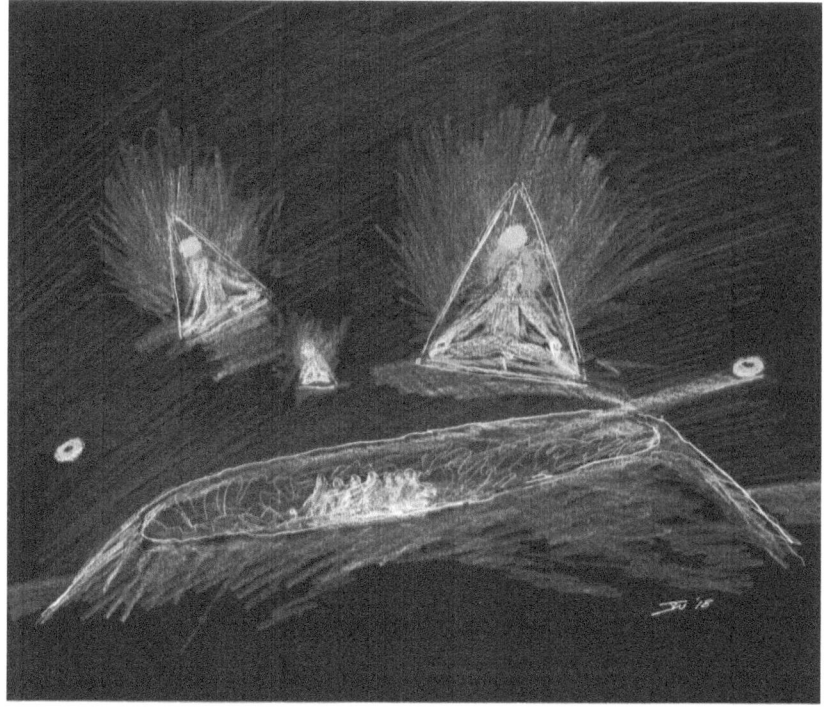

Little beings in pods of light fly around Silbury Hill. Credit: John Weaver.

The kids could see into the craft, which they referred to as "pods." In each one, they could make out a small humanoid, sitting in a lotus position with a sphere of orange light over its head. "They're little people!" one of them exclaimed.

They could not see details because the pods were self-illuminated and were glowing. The beings appeared to glow as you might imagine "beings of light" might – not reflected light from the ship, per se, but rather, light within themselves. The kids said they seemed to be little beings, about the size of children 4 to 5 feet tall. They couldn't tell anything more, except that the beings didn't appear to have clothes on.

They were thinking for a minute, *This is a joke! This is a military exercise. This is somebody who's got a projector going...* That sort of thing.

Sonya blinked her flashlight in the direction of the two little ships. Immediately, they turned towards the hill and floated towards them. Paul and Rob felt fear and terror, but Paul's fear abruptly vanished without explanation.

Meanwhile, the group of teenagers was fast asleep – they were "out" – and did not awaken.

The pods rose to about 10 feet over the witnesses and illuminated the area. Then they floated back down the hill, across the road and back into the field.

Car headlights were then seen coming up the A4 from the east, slowing as the vehicle approached the fog. Sonya thought she had some sort of a quasi-telepathic link with the inhabitants of the ships, because she could hear in her mind consternation and a kind of confusion, and a quick exchange of information, although she couldn't get any words. She felt they were trying to decide what to do, and quickly.

The mystery pods overlapped each other and collapsed into a single light about the size of a tennis ball, and hid in a hedgerow. Then it moved in behind the vehicle and briefly followed it. We found out later that the driver was another researcher, Paul Vigay, who observed the light following him and later reported it at a conference where he was a presenter.

The light then appeared back in the field to the east and across the A4 from Silbury Hill. Two beings came out, walked around, and got back in. The single light expanded and became a string of four or five lights, all of which moved off to a field to the southwest. Paul and Sonya had the impression that the lights were scanning the field as though they were searching for something. To Rob, the lights were laying out a gridwork of light in a pattern with little sparks that were emitted from some device that they were holding above the wheat in the field.

One of the teenagers, Jaime, awoke and heard the witnesses saying, "Oh wow! Jesus Christ! My God!" He was apparently "rooted" to the spot, seemingly unable to move until the very last minute when he thought, *My God. I've got to go over there.* He finally was able to join the three witnesses, and they all watched the lights fade and disappear.

I interviewed Jaime later, and he could not explain why he was unable to come over from the other side of the hill to where he saw glowing lights.

The whole sequence of events only lasted about 10-15 minutes.

After that fadeout, the other teens, who had seemingly been "anesthetized," got up and wordlessly left their stuff on top of the hill

Doe Kelly enjoys the energy in a crop circle near Silbury Hill. Credit: Ron Russell.

and stumbled down the hill. We've never been able to find any of them. I don't know who they were.

Paul, Sonya, Rob and Jaime spent the rest of the night on the hill. Rob was traumatized by this experience, and slept with lights on for about two years afterwards.

Now, our CSETI group had been on Silbury Hill just the night before. On the night the kids were there, we were on Windmill Hill, not far away, and we had spent nights along the ley line running through Avebury, Silbury Hill, and other nearby areas.

We were doing mental and light exercises using Dr. Steven Greer's protocols, trying to vector in extra-typical intelligence on ships known as UFOs for the benevolent purpose of communicating with them – just to say a simple "hello." Since this sort of thing probably had never been seen before in Britain, that is, luminous tetrahedral shapes with beings inside them, we thought maybe the work we had done during the previous six nights may have engendered this and opened a door to the Otherworld. We thought also that there may have been a connection with the ley line and the grids or scanning the beings were doing. We just don't know for sure.

Curiously, one of the methods we use to initiate a communication is a signal of a light that we flash into the sky. Interestingly, Sonya intuitively did that on her own, and she did get their attention.

After that, we sure kept our eye on the area. No crop formation showed up after the pods event, however, and within days the farmer cut the field.

The night I heard this story, my friends Mary Bennett and John and I went into that field to see if we could find the grid and perhaps have an experience. However, we were unable to get into the field, because we got sick at the effort. We were in the field next to it to approach it, and we all got waves of sickness that were very unpleasant. We left the field and tried to go back a few minutes later, thinking, *My gosh, what is this?*

Mary astutely insisted, "Look, this area is telling us *not* to do this! We had better just stay out of it!"

Within a day, British military came to the area with soldiers. They chased off a bread truck driver from the layby along the road right across from the hill, who was taking a nap at five in the morning. The soldiers parked in the same layby, took out electronic gear and went into the field with some kind of device. The bread truck driver couldn't explain it, but he thought it was like a TV camera on the end of a tall pole. The soldiers had many of these, with which they covered the whole area – the field where the pod lights seemed to have done their scanning.

Then that night, Mary, John and I returned to that field, and we had no difficulty at all; there was no energy there like that which had made us ill the night before.

In the subsequent year, I was in that very field across from Silbury Hill with Paul Vigay, Freddy Silva and Doe Kelly. I had taken a compass into a crop circle near where the beings from the year before were seen over the field. I showed Freddy, Paul and Doe how my analog compass needle was spinning around as I entered the formation, going faster as I moved toward the center. Paul had some gadgets and said the electromagnetic frequency was very high there, but he couldn't explain the spinning compass needle. We all said, "Wow!"

Pod Beings at Silbury Hill

Commentary

Silbury Hill is a Neolithic artificial chalk mound near Avebury in Wiltshire, the largest and oldest manmade mound in Europe. It is not far from Stonehenge, West Kennet Long Barrow (a burial mound), and the Avebury standing stones. It lies along the Michael ley line. Numerous crop circles have appeared around the hill. Its flat top once made it an ideal viewing platform for crop circle and UFO watchers, as well as a ritual platform for magical practitioners. Due to the fragility of the hill, climbing to the top of it today is prohibited, and violators face stiff fines.

There have been numerous documented accounts of eyewitnesses seeing mystery lights moving over the wheat fields of England, where most crop circles are formed, sometimes followed immediately by the appearance of an intricate crop circle. The area around Silbury Hill, Avebury and Stonehenge has been one of the most active in Wiltshire. The Silbury Hill "pod beings" event is one of the most, if not the most, unusual on record, with the details about the pod craft and the glowing beings inside them.

Many of England's crop circles have concentrated where powerful ley lines have been identified. Ley lines are alignments and patterns of invisible Earth energy said to connect and align sacred sites, such as churches, temples, stone circles, megaliths, holy wells, burial sites and other locations of spiritual or magical importance. Ley lines can be dowsed. Various theories of them have been advanced since the early 20th century, including that they were used by ancient peoples to construct sacred sites and tap into natural energy, or they are navigational aids for UFOs. In England, there are two major ley lines, the Michael and the Mary. The Michael line cuts diagonally across much of Britain, including straight through the heart of crop circle country.

Many crop circle enthusiasts have experimented with using mental powers to "call in" ET circlemakers, or use projected thought to manifest crop formations. Some groups have claimed success.

According to crop circle researcher Colin Andrews, a portal for craft exists in a field south of Silbury Hill, adjacent to the field where the witnesses saw the little people in their pods. Andrews was told by U.S. sources that, at the time of this event, both the U.S. and U.K. monitored the field on a 24/7 basis.

THE ALIEN EXAMINERS
Mary Grace O'Meara

A woman cooperates in her abduction by alien visitors, but her hopes for interaction are dashed.

I live along a river. It was the first week in August. I was walking through my garden after I'd finished watering, and I was on my way back to my cabin. I looked up and there stopped in mid-air was a spaceship.

It was twilight and I could still see. I looked up at the ship, and at first, I thought it was real neat. And then I got this strong feeling. There I was all alone, and they wanted me, so I ran into the cabin and locked the door. I didn't know how I knew that – I just had the feeling.

In the cabin, I was nervous and paced back and forth. I got my gun and put it by the chair. And then I figured, *Oh, what am I going to do with the gun?* So, I put the gun back.

I tried to turn on the radio, but it wouldn't work. I would have drunk a gallon of wine if I'd had it. Since I didn't have anything to drink,

I smoked a joint. That made things a little better. Then I went to the sink and drank a lot of water. I walked over to the window, and I saw this being on the other side.

He was about 4 to 4.5 feet tall. He was all white. He had a large head, and small – I mean really small – skinny arms, and small, skinny legs. He had long fingers for a little man, or whatever he was – they were longer than mine. He had big dark eyes, no nose, a little slit for a mouth, and no ears.

I was very frightened. I started crying and shaking. I guess I was in a mild state of shock.

I opened the window and asked him what he wanted. He told me telepathically that he wanted me to come outside. I felt compelled to obey, so I walked outside and stood there. Then he told me that he wanted me to go down the trail by my cabin. I followed him down the trail for about five minutes until we reached the ship.

All the while I was scared to death, but, oddly, I was cooperative. I felt a peaceful feeling, but at the same time, I was scared to death. I figured that they wouldn't hurt me.

Waiting outside of the ship were four others. They took me inside. I went into a corner.

They told me they wanted me to take off my clothes. I obeyed. They laid me on a table that popped up from the floor, and strapped this thing on my head. Tools and instruments simply appeared. I couldn't move. They examined me for what felt like about four hours or so. They just probed. I don't remember the whole examination, just bits and pieces of it, because I was so frightened.

The light was white and intensely bright. There were a lot of things that seemed to be real white, and they all had wires connected to them. The thing on my head was really weird, and hurt. They knew they were hurting me, but they didn't take it off, because I probably would have run out of there. It seemed to be the thing preventing me from moving. I was just like a dummy.

I felt intimidated, because they would not tell me a thing. I asked them who they were and where they were from. But they didn't tell me anything. I could tell that they were intelligent and were conversing back and forth among themselves, and they would only send messages to me that they wanted me to know. They probably were saying to each other, "Oh here's this human… let's get what we want…"

The whole time I was just like a guinea pig. I felt like a peon or a dog compared to them.

They conveyed that they wanted me to go away with them in their ship. At one time I might have done so because I was curious about aliens. They would not tell me where we would go, or that they would guarantee my passage back.

I told them I wouldn't mind going as long as I could come back. I didn't hear any answer, so I said, "I'm not going to go unless I can come back."

They accepted that and continued examining me. In retrospect, it was surprising – they could have forced me to go. But I guess the Earth is supposed to be a planet of free will.

After it was all over, I put my clothes on and they took me outside. I was so afraid, I could hardly move. I couldn't walk, and I told them they'd have to help me get home or I'd be there all night. So, they did. They sort of waddled me back home.

They left. They had no facial expressions, and there was no "see you later." No emotions.

Afterwards, I felt like I got ripped off. They went through my body inside and out and got a lot of information. I didn't even have a slice of information, where they were from, what they were doing, why they came to me – nothing.

We humans, especially the younger generation, think we can communicate with anybody. We'd be open and friendly. I've always had the feeling that if I ever encountered an alien, I could communicate. That I could say, "Let's communicate! Let's talk! Let's try to understand, because I'm probably interesting to you in some way, and you're interesting to me."

I could communicate with them, but they would not tell me anything about themselves. They had no desire to interact. Maybe because I didn't want to go.

So, I have to conclude that it's a myth that we can really be open and friendly, and expect that other beings will be receptive to us.

Commentary

Mary might count herself lucky to be merely disappointed by her encounter with alien beings – the majority of humans who wind up on a slab being probed have unpleasant to terrifying experiences. They describe themselves as feeling like a "lab rat," "a lower life form," "a specimen," "a guinea pig" (as Mary put it), and similar terms. In these scenarios, the aliens are not interested in communicating, except to manipulate the human subject, and they certainly aren't interested in getting-to-know-you-chitchat. People are forcefully taken or compelled to go along. The examinations make the victims feel vulnerable and helpless, and they are likely to be painful. If the aliens had wanted to take Mary away with them, they would have done so.

Not all alien encounters are frightening, however, and a small minority of reported abductions are not negative, either. On the other side of the coin, many experiencers say aliens are friendly and respectful, even loving, have personalities, and express an interest in forging a bond with human beings. It stands to reason that not all aliens would be the same, or have the same motives, just as all human beings are not uniform.

All things considered, Mary fared much better than many other abductees.

THE GRASS-EATING ALIENS
Jeanine Taicher

A woman recollects her bizarre childhood interactions with what she thinks are aliens and their craft, including a strange eating ritual.

I grew up in Belgium. When I was about 7 years old, I used to go into the fields to get some mushrooms and pick up rocks and such. I had an investigative mind as a child. I was even gathering crystals at that time, too.

One morning, I was out with my bike when I saw some lights that were flashing alternately like pulsar signals. A big craft was hovering and making a low noise, like a humming. The craft was not all the way down to the ground but almost down. Then it landed in a soccer field. It opened up with numerical sounds like a music box emanating from it.

I saw inside that it looked like an X-ray machine. There were three little aliens that came out really fast. The next minute they were sitting next to me. They looked at me. The best way I can describe them is

The aliens serve up a plate of grass. Credit: John Weaver.

that they looked like the aliens depicted by Betty and Barney Hill in their famous abduction case. They looked very skeletal, and on their hands and feet they had suction cups. Their eyes were round, whitish-greenish, like they had been in the ocean for ages.

    They were telling me to eat grass, and they had a silver plate with them. They put some grass on the plate. I looked at them, and I felt very loving and compassionate towards them, because they were very small and very skinny. I thought, *No wonder they are skinny, they just eat grass.* I was a child, so I was thinking as one.

    They did not handle the grass like a human being would, not as precisely. They didn't talk to me, but I understood what they meant. They were gentle and peaceful.

I looked at them and I said, "Do I have to eat grass?"

I had a feeling like a ripping of space and time, and suddenly I was sucked into the craft like a vacuum. It looked much bigger inside, and there were ridges and different compartments. It was like the inside of a vacuum tube.

They put machinery-like electrodes all over my head. Then I did not know any more. That was it. I cannot recall much more about it. I think I agreed to go along with them.

No one else was around. Somehow, I lost my bike, and it was never found. I think they took it, but I'm not sure. I would never have left my bike. The experience lasted about a whole day.

I recall that the craft looked like a tree upside down. There were three sides to it and it looked like a UFO. When I went under hypnosis later, I explained how the texture of the craft was like an embryo texture.

I had several other meetings with them when I was 9, and again at 10. After that, they did not come back.

Commentary

Childhood UFO and ET experiences are harder to evaluate than those that occur in adulthood. Many children dissociate easily into alternate realities filled with "imaginary" figures, and adults are likely to dismiss their extraordinary experiences as fantasy. However, many repeat alien contactees have their experiences start in childhood. For Jeanine, they did not extend into adulthood.

The UFO experiences of children cannot be dismissed out of hand, however. UFO researcher Cynthia Hind of South Africa documented many such cases. One of the most famous occurred in September 1994 in Zimbabwe, when a craft landed on a school grounds while 62 children ages 5 to 12 were outside playing. A small humanoid about 3 feet in height appeared on top of the craft. The "little man" had a scrawny neck, long black hair, and huge eyes. He walked a short way across the ground toward the students. When he noticed the children, he vanished and then reappeared at the back of the object. The object then took off and vanished.

Some of the younger children were afraid the being was a demon that would eat them. Some of the older ones said they were given telepathic messages that humans are destroying the planet at our peril.

The grass eating in Jeanine's case is reminiscent of another strange food-related ET episode that occurred in April 1961 to an adult male, Joe Simonton of Eagle River, Wisconsin. Simonton was having a late breakfast in his home when he heard a sound outside like a jet throttling back. He went outside and saw a flying saucer hovering over his farm. It was silver and "brighter than chrome," and about 12 feet in height and 30 feet in diameter. On one edge were what appeared to be exhaust pipes 6 or 7 inches in diameter.

The disc landed, and a hatch opened. Inside were three dark-skinned humanoid aliens, each about 5 feet tall and weighing about 125 pounds, Simonton estimated. They appeared to be between 25 and 30 years old (in Earth years) and were dressed in dark blue or black knit uniforms with turtleneck tops, and helmet-like caps. They were clean-shaven and "Italian-looking."

The beings had a silver-colored jug with two handles, and conveyed by telepathy that they wanted water. Simonton obliged, filling the jug in his basement. When he returned to the craft to hand it over, he was able to look inside, where he saw one of the beings apparently cooking pancakes on a flameless appliance.

The alien who seemed to be in charge gave him three pancakes right off the griddle, and they took off in their craft and quickly disappeared. The pancakes were about 3 inches in diameter and perforated with little holes. Simonton ate one; it tasted like cardboard. (No wonder the aliens wanted water.)

He gave the other two pancakes to a local judge, who in turn gave them to the National Investigations Committee on Aerial Phenomena (NICAP), which declined the case. J. Allen Hynek became involved, and had the Air Force test the pancakes. They were said to be composed of hydrogenated fat, starch, buckwheat hulls, soy bean hulls, and wheat bran, and had no abnormal bacteria or radiation readings. The Food and Drug Laboratory of the U.S. Department of Health, Education and Welfare concluded that the material was an ordinary pancake of terrestrial origin.

Simonton was ridiculed in the media, but the case remains unexplained.

Another famous case involving food – this time in the form of pills – was that of Carl Higdon, a 41-year-old oil driller who lived in Wyoming, in 1974. On October 25, Higdon went out alone to hunt elk. He changed *his destination when he came upon some hunters who advised him that the best hunting was in a remote region of the Medicine Bow National Forest.*

Late in the afternoon, Higdon aimed his new 7mm Magnum rifle at a large elk and pulled the trigger. To his astonishment, there was no sound or kickback. Even more astonishing, he watched the bullet travel through the air in slow motion and then fall into the snow.

As he examined the oddly-misshapen bullet, he suddenly became aware of the presence of a man-like being that definitely was not human. It stood over 6 feet tall and was dressed in an outfit resembling a wet scuba suit with a harness, a yellow, six-pointed star and some sort of symbol. There was no chin, and the slit-like mouth revealed three huge teeth. The skin was yellowish. The legs were bowed and the arms exceptionally long; the right one ended in a drill-like bit instead of a hand.

The creature walked toward him and said in English, "How you doin'?" as though he was a long-lost friend.

It then asked Higdon if he was hungry, and before the hunter could answer, a cellophane-like package floated toward him:

> He [the alien] waved a pointed object where his right hand should have been, and it levitated over to me. I opened the packet and found four pills inside. He told me, in English, to take one of them. That it would last four days. Now normally I don't like taking pills, not even an aspirin, but something happened. It's as if I had no control over my actions. So, I just swallowed one of them, and put the other three into my jacket pocket.

Ausso One, as the alien introduced himself, proceeded to abduct Higdon aboard a craft. Actually, it was an invitation to come aboard, but, like the offers made by the mob, it was an invitation that could not be refused.

There Higdon saw other beings like Ausso One, as well as five human beings plus five paralyzed elk. They were told they were being taken to a planet 163,000 "light miles" from Earth. The humans were scanned by some sort of device, and Higdon was informed he was being taken back to his own planet. He had the impression the aliens were interested in a breeding program, and he had failed the cut.

They dumped him back in the forest and he made his way back to his pickup truck. In the aftermath, Higdon was examined at a hospital. It was discovered that his kidney stones had miraculously disappeared.

He underwent hypnosis. He said that for weeks after his experience, he was tracked by "a colossal green light" in the sky, and felt like a tagged bear.

The three pills that Higdon put in his jacket pocket mysteriously disappeared.

The sharing of food to establish friendship and community is one of the oldest and most universal customs on Earth. Is it so with alien beings from other places – or do some of them know of our customs and make use of them for their own advantage? Is there a Trickster side to it?

In fairy lore – as we have discussed, there are many similarities between fairies and ETs – eating food offered by fairies is a risky thing to do. According to lore, if one is abducted or finds his way to fairyland – a twilight alternate reality – one should not eat the food offered, no matter how tempting, or the person will be trapped forever in fairyland. Another piece of lore holds that food left as offerings for the fairies – who consume the vital life essence from it – is then not fit for man or beast, and will make people and animals ill if they eat it.

ET cases involving food have not seemed to be linked to the exact same consequences, but perhaps the consuming of food with aliens, or offered by aliens, establishes an energetic link that may be used by them later. Jeanine, after her grass experience, had other encounters with the aliens, and Higdon felt watched and tracked. Simonton apparently had no ill effects from his pancake.

Follow-up encounters happen to experiencers without any involvement of food, so it is obvious the aliens don't need food to make a connection. It may be that in offering food to humans, they are seeking to gain trust for whatever are their purposes – which seldom pans out in the favor of the humans. Just like the fairies.

ABDUCTED BY INSECTOIDS
Jim G.

A man has a terrifying bedroom encounter with a praying mantis being and its beetle-like companion, followed by abductions.

In April 2001, I was living in a small town on the outskirts of London. I can't recall the exact day or date, because for a long time I tried to deny to myself it ever happened.

I woke up at about 2:30 in the morning to find a tall praying mantis-looking being and a cloaked being by the side of my bed. I thought to myself, *What crazy dream is this?*

The cloaked being looked at me from beneath its hood, revealing black skin, which appeared leathery and reflected light much like a beetle's skin.

I shut my eyes, thinking this must be a realistic dream! But when I re-opened my eyes, the figures were unfortunately still there. The cloaked figure looked up to the tall praying mantis type, as if it was confused as

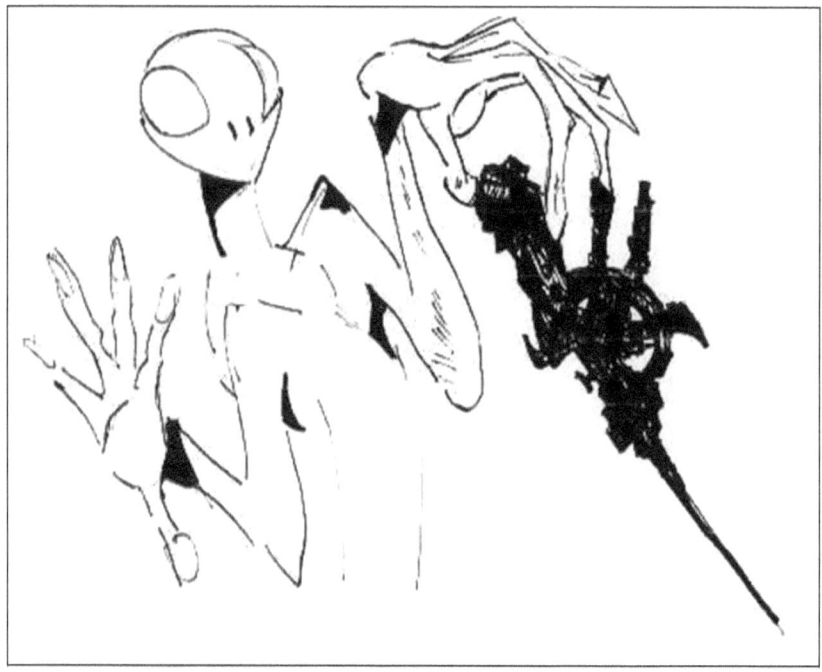
Praying mantis being with needle-like object. Credit: Jim G.

to what actions it should take next. The praying mantis turned its head towards the hooded one and made a series of high-pitched clicking sounds. I sensed this was the one in command, and possibly the other was a security guard.

It was at this point that I realized, *I'm definitely not dreaming.* I could hear them. I couldn't move, and my brain went into a deep panic. *Oh my God what is going on? What are they?*

I didn't want to look too closely at the mantis, so I just glanced at it. All I recall was that it was tall. At least 7 feet, as it had to bend its neck because of the height of the ceiling. Its head was pointed with large eyes. Its forearms were extremely long and moved in a jerky fashion.

The cloaked figure was closer, crouching by my bed, so I couldn't tell how tall it was. I could clearly see that it was wearing some kind of over-lapping ridged armor, including a metallic-looking breastplate that had a series of circles on it. Its head was dome-like with emotionless facial features. Its eyes were large and surrounded by detailed ridges. It acted in a way that reminded me of a robot or insect.

I thought to myself, *Nobody is going to believe this! A bloody giant-sized mantis and medieval-style dressed alien, what the hell is this?*

The mantis bent its upper body over my bed and directly above me. In its hand it was holding a long metal object that looked like a needle. A green light shot directly from the needle into my right eye. Maybe it was a laser, I was not sure, but I do know it felt very painful. I could see all the veins in my eye – the same effect you get when an optician checks your eyes.

I screamed but no noise came out. I then felt something stick into my skull! I'm not sure what it was because by that time I had my eyes closed. I pretended to sleep and went into deep panic! My mind was racing at a million miles per hour. I heard a great *whooshing* sound and when I next opened my eyes, thankfully they had gone.

I lay shaking and confused for what seemed like hours, and could not return to sleep.

At no time did I feel like they cared about my health or me! They seemed to have an insect, cold type of mentality. I really thought I was going to die. The next day I spent the whole day in bed and felt as if I had been through a major operation.

I was in shock for a long while afterwards. It is very painful to recall. Since this incident, I sometimes hear clicking sounds inside my head.

Before this incident, I was familiar with the gray types of aliens, though I had not seen one, but I had never heard of the praying mantis types. I can say that this definitely happened, this definitely was real. I have no answers or conclusion, but I think it's important to get real-life accounts out there.

[For several years, Jim G. released lengthy updates on his experiences. He began to feel that the experiences were causing Post Traumatic Stress Disorder (PTSD). An abridgement follows.]

2003

The day after the incident in 2001, I did do a word search on "mantis-type aliens" and got nothing. Although I knew it did happen, I really just put it down to a very realistic dream and denied it to myself until six months ago.

After a little research I realized that these were well-defined aliens within ufology. If other people were seeing what I'd seen, then either it was a coincidence or it's really happening!

Why do I think they chose me? Well, I've had many of what a lot of people would describe as strange experiences while I was a kid, (seeing UFOs, the walls talking to me every birthday) but I think a lot of kids have these things happen.

I was 18 years old in the summer of 1992, and while working in London, I sneezed, and a metal ball fell out of my left nostril! I now suspect it was an implant.

In the summer of 1996, it was a real hot night, so I thought I'd climb out of my bedroom window and on to the roof of my house. I got the strangest feeling of being watched. I looked into the star-filled night sky and had the crazy thought of trying to communicate with aliens telepathically. It felt right somehow. I just sent out feelings of love and that if anyone could pick this up, I'd like to communicate.

Way up high, a ball of light appeared. I assumed it to be a satellite until it turned, dived and hovered 200 feet above me. I could clearly see it was a ball of light. It made no sound whatsoever. I stared in utter amazement. I felt calm and euphoric, completely at one with the world. The ball then just disappeared. I climbed back into my bedroom and fell into a deep sleep.

Since then, I started to have really strange experiences. I'd wake up in the middle of night floating above my bed! One time I even floated outside my house and in the distance, I could see the ball of light and I was getting pulled towards it. I imagined myself surrounded by white light and I flew back to my bed with a thud. I don't think I was astral projecting, this felt real.

So, I'm really not sure why they chose me. Maybe they sensed a spiritual awakening within me, or more likely, it was just mere opportunity.

They just spotted some young fool on a roof of a house and thought, *He'll do, easy pickings.* One thing is for sure – I felt no spiritual vibes or energy from these beings at all. I just felt like a lab rat.

One of the more significant incidents happened on November 10, 2003.

For the sake of my own sanity more than anything, I was convinced that I could get some solid evidence. The plan was simple: grab something off one of the beings.

Around 3 AM, I was lying in my bed, half-asleep, when I heard a noise in my bedroom. It was like "someone" was stealthily walking across my bedroom carpet. I pretended to be asleep and waited.

A few seconds later, I heard the noise again; this time there was no mistaking it, there was something walking towards me.

I waited a little longer then jumped out of my bed. Everything went into slow motion. As my quilt went flying across the room, before it even landed, something squealed! (in surprise?) I can only describe it as like a high-pitched electronic pig squeal!

The "something" ran away from me at high speed, knocking into some small storage boxes on the floor.

I landed on my feet and put my arms up into a fighting position, but it was so dark my eyes could barely adjust to the darkness. I could just make out a humanoid figure wearing a dark bluish cloak running towards the back of the corridor part of my bedroom.

I kept my eyes firmly on the cloaked being, which was in a hunched position, staring back at me from the far side of the corridor. It was between 4 and 5 feet tall and wearing a dark hooded robe which looked as if it was covered in a purple-bluish energy (liquid in appearance).

I relaxed as much as I could and changed my hands from clenched fists to open palms. I said as calmly as possible, "I'm not going to fight you."

No reply.

I then asked, "What are you?"

Again no reply. Its hooded head was pointing in my direction and I could barely just make out two reddish eyes. The being then got up, ignored me, turned and walked into and through the wall! As it disappeared from sight, it looked up at me from beneath its hood. I could clearly see two reddish-blackish eyes stare at me.

I didn't go back to sleep but stayed up all night constantly questioning what had just occurred. I took the next day off sick. I felt drained.

I think it was the cloaked being that I saw with the praying mantis alien in my first incident but I'm not sure. Looking back on it, this seemed to be the catalyst for the increased alien activities that happened afterward.

On December 18, I was staying at my brother's house. I slept in the spare bedroom. I fell asleep at around 12:30 AM.

Without any warning I found myself wide-awake and completely unable to move! The clicking sound was continually screeching in my head. I screamed but no sound came out from my mouth.

With every muscle I could muster, I pushed myself up on my side and turned my head to the bottom of the bed.

Standing before me was a tall mantis-like being! The same mantis being I had seen before. The terror I felt was completely overwhelming. The only way I can describe it is, it feels like waves of fear washing over you.

It was wearing a long dark robe. It was about 7-plus feet tall and vaguely humanoid. The body was extremely bony and skinny with a long black snake-like neck. Its head was grayish blackish and triangular in shape, reminding me of a skull. The eyes were bulbous, black and rounded with a liquid-like appearance. In fact, everything on the mantis was liquidy looking, like oil shimmering in the sun.

The arms were extremely long with multiple joints extending out in a "messiah pose," like a human with outstretched "come-to-me" arms. The forearms were bent forward longer than the rest of the arm.

As soon as it noticed me, the mantis, with extreme speed, extended huge bony legs from beneath its robe and ran directly into and through the wall! Its feet made a clunking sound as it ran across the floor, confirming this was a solid object moving through the room! The way this skeletal alien moved was jerky and fast, like a huge scuttling beetle.

As it ran through, I could see a strange red glow where it's body came in contact with the wall. At the same time, a door to a built-in wardrobe on the same wall rattled loudly as if it was hit by an energy field.

Beetle-like cloaked being. Credit: Jim G.

2004

I don't know what's going on but can assure you these aren't dreams; something real is happening to me. This happens about twice a week (but I can stop completely for say a month, if I'm lucky).

A typical scenario starts with me lying in bed. Just as I'm about to fall asleep, I hear a high-pitched clicking sound inside my head. Within a few minutes I hear the same sound again but this time it is *inside* my bedroom.

Before I pass out, through half shut eyes, I see a reddish glow appear on my far wall, followed by shadowy movements of tall figures coming out of the light towards me. I always try my best to fight it and stay conscious, but it never works, and I always lose consciousness.

The next day I'm completely exhausted. My whole body aches all over as though it has been through a major operation. Sometimes my body is covered in bruises. In August 2003, I woke up to find five separate bruises on the inner thigh of my right leg. The bruises made up a wide spreading imprint in the shape of a huge hand.

On January 16, in the middle of the night I suddenly found myself wide-awake. A loud buzzing sound filled my ears. I was curled up on my bed in a fetal position facing the closest wall. I felt a force push on the back of my head. I wouldn't say it hurt exactly but it was extremely uncomfortable.

Again, I heard the loud clicking sound in my head. This time it panned from my right ear to the left. I looked at my arm; it was covered in a bluish-purplish pulsating energy. I couldn't move my legs or arms. I found I could just about move my head.

Somehow, I managed to break free and used all my effort to turn around. Standing before me in the center of my bedroom was a short humanoid creature, with a large mantis/fly-looking head. A beam of energy was coming from the alien to me.

I felt I had known this being all my life. I also felt that I'd been manipulated into feeling this.

The creature was humanoid and 5 feet 5 inches tall. I made a mental note where it's head came up on my wardrobe and measured it the next day. Its head was huge in relation to its body. Its eyes were extremely large, shiny, insect-like and were supported by big sockets. My first impressions were that it looked like a cross between a praying mantis and a fly. This being did not look like the tall praying mantis beings, and was surrounded by a bluish-purplish energy. In the center of its cloak was a golden badge. I looked closer at its head; it had two protrusions between the eyes and a mass of protrusions where a mouth would normally be.

[Jim described an experience in which he was taken somewhere and was with insect-like beings who despised humanity. They were engaged in a secret

agenda, which he described as "sinister." He was shown a 3-D hologram of Earth and given information about different countries, including America, and he communicated with a disembodied male-sounding voice.]

I was shown a deep underground military base with seven circular levels, connected by a vertical shaft. On the seventh and largest level I was shown a cross-section revealing humans working with gray aliens and large praying mantis aliens.

There were literally thousands of aliens; I saw a figure that seemed to imply around 14,000 aliens in this base. If this is to be believed, not only do aliens exist, but they also seem to be very well established on Earth. The base was somewhere in a desert.

The male voice said, "We have tried to communicate with them in the past, but they lie to us and try to use us. You kill what you do not understand. You humans are still so un-evolved."

I tried to argue, "Some of us are trying to evolve but we have to fight the ones that aren't so evolved, not because we're cruel, but because they want to kill us!" The voice didn't seem interested in having a debate.

On March 14, I woke up to see two of the tall praying mantis types standing in the middle of my room. They looked as if they were engaged in a conversation, making high-pitched (almost digital) clicking sounds at each other. Both were extremely thin and tall, well over 7 feet high. One was slightly taller than the other. Their necks were long, flexible and tube-like, and did not look strong enough to support the triangular heads.

Both were wearing long black robes that again looked like liquid oil. On the side of the face I could clearly see a small round hole just below their eyes.

I felt completely drained and couldn't move. The fear and trauma I've experienced is getting to be too much. I'm dealing with it because I've got no choice. I don't know what's going on or what they want.

It seems to happen in phases. I try to avoid sleeping between 2 and 4 in the morning, but obviously I don't keep it up for too long. I end up falling asleep and that's when they come. I do feel that I've got an implant and it is a monitoring device, to what extent I can't say.

2005

I've found a way of escaping the abductions, simply by spending more time in inner London. I think it makes it harder for them to mount an operation in a populated area. Maybe I'm not that important to them to take the risk, but for whatever reason, I feel safe in inner London.

[By April 2008, Jim reported that he was still suffering from Post Traumatic Stress Disorder, and he still had occasional nightmares, but the attacks and abductions had subsided. He thought the reason was his move to London and immersion in an urban environment. He slept with lights on. If he thought too much about his experiences, he became overwhelmed and numb.]

Commentary

Aliens resembling praying mantises appear in many abduction accounts, and experiencers describe them as "overseers" and "in charge." They loom over people in their beds, causing extreme fright.

On the flip side of the coin, some contactees and abductees describe the praying mantis beings as highly evolved, benevolent, and full of healing energy. They are said to be assisting with alien-human hybrid programs, and hundreds of thousands of "mantis souls" are already incarnate on the Earth.

If Jim was part of a hybrid program, he had no conscious recollection of it. But all his experiences were negative, including the ability of the beings to manipulate his emotions. Other abductees have had similar experiences with manipulated emotions, even feeling "love" for the aliens.

Like many abductees, Jim was at a loss for the reason why the beings targeted him as a "lab rat." The evidence indicates that perhaps he had been "tagged" much earlier in life, in the way humans tag animals in the wild to study them. Other abductees fit this pattern. His rooftop attempt to establish contact may have escalated the aliens' involvement.

Whatever their reasons, the aliens commenced their activities abruptly and ceased just as abruptly, and without reason.

The dark side of contact has been well documented for several decades, and many abductees have undergone hypnosis to recover more information about their experiences. Some say their trauma has been worth it, that they have gained some knowledge or "understanding" in the process. Critics speculate this is the "Stockholm Syndrome," a survival mechanism in which victims form a psychological alliance with their captors/tormenters.

An increasing number of positive contact experiences have been reported, which balances the picture of human-alien involvement. Where does the truth lie? No one knows.

ALIEN MACHINE SHOP 101
Karl Petry

A man who is a psychic medium is repeatedly taken aboard an alien craft to provide information about the mechanics of Earth vehicles and machinery.

All my life I've had experiences where I am pulled out of my sleep and taken somewhere to watch something or participate in something. These experiences are like lucid dreams, except they are real, physical, and real-time. Usually they involve the dead, and I have had time travels into the past. Since 2015, I've had an increasing number of experiences involving aliens.

Around July 20, 2017, some alien experiences started that went on nightly for two weeks.

I would be trying to sleep and suddenly find myself inside a spaceship that was huge inside. I would witness aliens zap up cars, trucks and machinery into the craft and then start to disassemble them, as though they were trying to figure out how they worked. They were going all over the world, taking vehicles and machines and tools.

I felt as though I was seeing through their eyes. They communicated with each other by telepathy, but I noticed that as they handled each part, I would think, "This is a bolt," "This is a drive shaft," and so on, and it occurred to me that I was identifying parts for them. I'm pretty skilled as a mechanic.

The aliens were tall grays. I'm 6-3, and judged them to be about 5-8. Their hands were like ours but thinner and with much longer fingers. Their skin was a light sickly gray color, and they were dressed in blue-green uniforms made out of some kind of shiny material like satin.

They lifted up whatever they wanted by a beam that came from the ceiling of the craft. I saw a four-cylinder car taken from France, and when the beam turned off it slammed on the floor and I could hear the metal shake.

They opened the car door and looked inside and then seated themselves looking at the dashboard in total amazement as if they couldn't believe it. They wanted to take it apart, but they couldn't because they didn't have tools. They went to a garage near where they had taken the car, and zapped up tools in boxes on wheels, like you would find in a machine shop.

They started taking the car apart. They would hold every part in their hands and look at it and then take another part off. They were interested in the tires, but confused by them. They realized they were filled with air, which really amazed them.

They also worked on some Earth machines I could not identify; one looked like it rolled large sheets of metal. They also had a tractor truck.

I had the feeling that they had been doing this for quite a while – taking machines and cars. They never reassembled anything, and they never returned anything. They had no interest in electronics – no televisions, radios, computers. They were interested in mechanical things.

They were full of wonderment and curiosity. We think of ETs as sophisticated and light years ahead of us in technology, but our cars, combustion engines and machines were amazing to them. Maybe they had a need for moving things around on the surface of the Earth, and whatever they have was not as good as what we have.

I noticed they had a strong negative reaction to gasoline. I don't know if it was just unpleasant to them or toxic and dangerous, but if they smelled gas, they were repulsed. They also didn't like getting grease on their hands, but it wasn't the same recoil as gasoline.

This observation didn't stop at night for me. During the day, I would be going along and get sudden intrusions of visions that picked up where I'd left off at night. This went on and on.

Since I could look out through their eyes, I sensed their knowledge of their superiority to humans. They are so advanced compared to us. But they gave us respect for coming up with steel and aluminum and engines.

After two weeks, the experiences stopped, but now they go in spurts. I won't have any for a while, and then I will have a cluster of them. Same thing.

I've had two other unusual encounters with aliens. In 2008, when those lights and craft were sighted over Stephenville, Texas, I was taken aboard the ship along with some other Earth people. The ship was about 3 to 4 stories high. I was at the edge of the ship looking down and could see everything that they – the aliens – could see. Even though we were high up in the sky, it was like we were down close to ground level. Everything was transparent. I could see people in their cars, houses, even behind trees. I realized that there was no way to hide from them. If they want to take you, they will and there's nothing you can do about it. It was a real eye-opener for me. I could not see the aliens, but I knew they were there. It seemed like they wanted us all to know, *Don't even think about trying to hide from us, because we can see you wherever you are.* It wasn't a threat, but a show of power.

In 2015, I started getting downloads of mathematical formulas while I was trying to go to sleep. It was like a blackboard appeared in front of me and would be covered with equations, which then flashed off and were replaced by other equations. I have no background in math and had no idea what they meant, or why I was getting them. That happened for two nights in a row.

Commentary

The endless dismantling of primitive machines to see how they work makes little sense; but then, so many phenomena related to alien encounters defy the "rules" of logic. How many cars, cows and people do the aliens need to probe or take apart? If Karl served a function to name parts, why didn't the aliens put the information into their own "product manuals" for further reference, instead of repeating the same activities over and over again?

Karl is not the only contactee to get mathematical formulas that are incomprehensible or, if remembered and written down, make little sense. Likewise, contactees with no medical training are given the cure for cancer and so on, but have no way of moving the information into society. Again, there is a Trickster element, for if the aliens wanted to put certain information into the heads of humans, they would select people who could comprehend the information and do something with it.

The implied message from the Stephenville ship is ominous, however. We humans can run but we cannot hide; resistance is futile. Are they biding their time, waiting for a perfect moment?

A NIGHT LIKE NO OTHER
Karen Lake

Alien visitations change a woman's life.

In 2001, I was working in a casino in the state of Idaho. November 1 was my night off work. I went to bed at around 10 PM. At exactly 2:30 AM I awoke and saw the clock on the dresser. Then I looked at the foot of my bed and there I saw three aliens known to me as the grays.

I tried to get out of bed but could not move a muscle, except to turn my head. I felt frantic, like I was trapped. I could feel the beings working on me, or whatever it is they do. Something was inserted into my left ear and it felt like a hornet buzzing around, which was really strange.

I don't know how long all this lasted but the next thing I knew my vision changed into a kaleidoscope vision with colors of greens and whites. This was a lot calmer on me than the hornet buzzing in my ear.

I don't know how long they worked on me, but I knew I was chosen for some reason. The reason has not yet been shared with me to this day.

I awoke some time later, jumped out of bed and ran to the windows to look out at the forest. Everything looked so natural, a beautiful landscape of some of Idaho's greatest mountain beauty.

I tried the door to make sure it was locked, and it was. Now how did they get inside? I don't know how they could have done it, but there they were!

I picked up the phone to call a psychic friend of mine. I asked him about the experience and he told me that I was being prepared to help out in the last days of Mother Earth as we know it. This did not sit well with me, but I trusted my friend's opinion. I accepted what he told me.

During this time, I was getting ready to go to Nashville to sign papers with a record company for my first song. I went to work, finished the week and prepared for my trip.

I noticed at work that I felt kind of spacey. This continued and I knew I had to seek medical treatment. I just wouldn't share the alien experience with anyone, especially the medical field.

After I returned home from Nashville, I went back to work, a little tired out but filled with much enthusiasm. I had not been on a nice vacation in several years. The spacey feeling returned and some days I had a hard time standing up. My speech got a little blurry at times.

One day my boss sent me home and told me to get to a doctor as he figured something was wrong – and it was. My blood pressure was sky high. They gave me high blood pressure pills and took me off work a couple of days to rest.

I went back to work a little more rested. Some days it would be normal readings and other days my blood pressure would be sky high again. All the while though I had a fear of the aliens coming back to mess with me again or hurt me. I was too shy about talking to others about my feelings. Most people didn't know a thing about aliens, let alone someone who had been worked on. I had a couple close friends who I was able to communicate my feelings to.

I listened to *Coast to Coast AM* on the radio, and one night I got on and told my story. George Noory said he believed me. That gave me a little more confidence in talking about my experience.

Winter turned to spring and spring turned to summer. I was supposed to do hairstyles for a wedding. I made it through the hairstyles and the beautiful wedding. I left the wedding and drove the 20 miles to go to work. I finally got off work, and had two days off.

I awoke the next morning at 11 AM. I felt like I had been run over by a herd of wild horses. Everywhere in my body I hurt. I made it through the day.

The next morning, I woke up and I felt very sick, so I went to take a shower. I was getting out and drying off and I felt a ping in my head above my left ear. It didn't hurt until a minute later, then it was like I had 50 headaches on top of each other.

I threw on my jeans and sweat shirt and ran to the neighbor's house. I was screaming at the top of my lungs. The pain was horrible. My neighbor rushed me down to the clinic. They figured I had a brain aneurysm and rushed me by ambulance to Spokane, Washington.

I was in the ambulance waiting to go into the hospital when I found myself outside my body and the ambulance and in the sky and clouds. It felt great to be out of pain. I lingered there awhile, not caring if I made it back to my body. I saw my mom and spoke with her.

I was in and out of my coma for three days. On the third day I heard a male voice tell me it wasn't my time to die. I felt special like I had a purpose for the rest of my life.

The nurse came in and I asked her where the doctor went. She said there hasn't been a doctor in this morning. I told her I heard a male voice tell me it wasn't my time to die.

She touched my shoulder and said, "Sweetie that was God. I hear this all the time." She smiled and told me the kind of aneurysm I had is survived by only 1 out of 3000 people. "You are one of the lucky ones," she said. That left me with a feeling of great satisfaction. I knew now how important life really is now since I almost died.

I knew I was strong, but this was proving to be too much. The days in the hospital went by fast. I was able to return home after staying with my daughter for a week and my dad for five days.

Getting back home was great but I had a lot of ups and downs. The weeks flew by and turned to months and years! I had to learn to read again, and it took me six years to read a book.

Then I landed a job with that Nashville record company, and that was a great chance for me to help get my music going. I loved to write songs, poetry and articles. I interviewed the stars in the country music field.

I believe my brain aneurysm was a result of whatever the aliens did to me that first night they came. I don't think they intended to harm me – it was an accidental effect.

After a couple years of no other alien encounters, I started to relax a little more and wasn't near as skittish. One night, though, I had an experience I shall never forget.

I was coming home from a friend's house, and it was about midnight. My son and his wife were staying with me for the summer and I wanted to get home to them. I had to get up early to be at work.

I was on a lonely mountain road, and as I came close to Wind Fall Pass Road, I noticed what I thought to be the full moon, large and bright in the sky. As I got closer I decided it was not the full moon as it was just above tree level.

I pulled my car to the side of the road and flashed my head lights on and off four times. All at once the circular bright light started down the horizon ahead of me. It disappeared and then it appeared, all at once again. As the bright light came back towards me, I put my car in gear to make it home. It swirled around doing maneuvers I had never before witnessed. I was very excited and scared.

I was only a couple miles from home. I continued driving my car down the road, all the while watching as the bright light put on a light show I shall never forget nor have witnessed since that night. As I drove down the road and the last curve before reaching my driveway the bright light disappeared ahead of me in the trees.

I drove up my driveway and saw my daughter-in-law sitting on the deck. She came running out to the car and said, "Where is the other car?"

"There is no other car," I said, "but wait till you see what followed me home." I pointed to the circular light again at tree level above us.

Her eyes grew big as she said, "Is that what I think it is?"

I nodded my head yes.

She said just before I returned home the driveway and trees lit up. She thought it was me coming, but no car appeared. When I did arrive, she thought the bright light was another car.

The bright light in the sky hovered above my home till dawn, and when I got up to get ready for work, it had disappeared. I thought it was the aliens checking up on me. I did not feel bad that it was gone.

It just made me so much more curious as to what had happened, and "Why Me"!

Unfortunately, I didn't have my camera with me to take photos, but the experience is embedded in my brain I feel forever!

The years have passed by and I still have these memories like it all happened yesterday.

I always want to know the details of why this happened and what I am supposed to do with the experience. I love to write, so maybe my experiences will make it easier for others who have experienced these beings or UFO sightings to understand that they are not alone, as this is a worldwide phenomenon. I just tell myself there must have been a purpose for what I've gone through. I will do what I can to help or teach others.

Commentary

Karen Lake is among many contactees who have had health complications arising from their interactions with aliens. In Karen's case, she did not feel the complications were deliberately caused, but an accidental by-product. Perhaps the aliens do not understand enough about human physiology.

More significant were other changes: an increase in creativity, and a new sense of having a purpose in the advancement of human consciousness. These, too, are reported by other contactees.

THE BORREGO SPRINGS CONTACT
Norman Wayne Garcia

Aliens contact a woman on a radio and direct her to meet them at a designated place.

In 1968, there was a big UFO flap, a wave of sightings. This happened to my mother, Basilisa Oguita Garcia near San Diego. She apparently got contacted by aliens through her little radio that she had.

She listened to her radio almost every night, and at least three times a week she got these messages from aliens. She would not hear them like a radio broadcast. Rather, the radio seemed to serve as a medium, and the messages were impressed in her head. She would go out on the patio and look up at the stars and just sit out there while the rest of us were sleeping. She had four of us kids, so she was sort of getting away from it all.

She would make comments like, "There's going to be a UFO sighting at such and such place."

One night, she was out there listening to the radio, and she got some kind of communication with a UFO. She was told, "We've been watching you," or something to that effect. They said they would like to contact her in person, and they would give her directions to the place where their next sighting or landing would be, where they could be met. Mom had to do something else, and for one reason or another, we could not get to that place.

She got more messages. This one particular time, they said that they were going be out in Borrego Springs in the desert. They said that they'd like to contact her there, and, if possible, take her up into their UFO with them. She said she would try to make it there.

Mom talked my father into going and bringing us, too, out there just for the weekend. She said to my father, "Well, the reason that we're going is that I've been contacted by the UFO people, and they want me to go aboard their ship."

But my dad said, "What if they never bring you back?"

She answered, "No, I don't think they'll do that."

Then he said, "Well, what about the kids? If they don't bring you back, what am I supposed to do with them?"

So, she began to have second thoughts about it all. But, my father believed her, and agreed to take us all out to the state park in Borrego Springs. Mom didn't explain much about it to us kids, except my older sister and me.

On the way to Borrego Springs, Mom still had second thoughts about whether she wanted to meet the aliens.

When we arrived in the area, there was a little general store. Mother walked up to the guy behind the counter and asked, "Where do you usually sight your UFOs?"

The guy started laughing and said, "What are you talking about, lady?"

Mother said, "I'm serious. Where do you usually see them?"

He replied, "Well, we don't usually see them, so don't ask me anymore."

She said, "Okay, then."

She walked over to the ranger station in the park and asked the man there the same question. This guy, too, started laughing, just like the guy in the general store.

We pitched our tent to stay the night there. Around 9 o'clock, when the littler kids were asleep, mother asked my older sister, if she would have the chance, would she want to come with her?

My sister said, "Sure!"

All of a sudden, my mom got some kind of message in her brain that said, "We're here, and we're going to come for you."

My dad was asleep by then. Mom said, "Well, I have second thoughts about it, and I'm not really sure if you guys will bring me back."

They said, "We will."

But she still couldn't trust them, because she'd never really met them. She stared out in the desert, and the only things she could see were two or three very large tumbleweeds coming towards her. There was something odd and weird about the tumbleweeds, though, that were different from other tumbleweeds.

Mom was getting scared. She said, "No, I can't make it."

They said, "We understand."

She hid herself in the bottom of the sleeping bag, and she stuffed my sister down there with her too.

That was the end of it.

The next morning when we woke up, there was a big hubbub going on about something that had happened in the desert during the night. When Mom asked somebody, they said, "Didn't you see it? There was a spaceship out there, just sitting out there, for the longest time."

She said, "No, we didn't see it."

They said, "Well, it's in the newspaper here. You can get it at the general store."

She then went over to the general store, and as she walked in, the guy who had laughed at her said, "Well, what'd they say?"

"What are you talking about?" she said.

"The UFO guys... What did they say?"

She said, "I didn't see any UFOs."

He said, "Ah, come on, you know, you had to see them, they were right out there. It says so in the papers!"

"Can I see the paper?"

He replied, "No, this one's mine, and I want to keep it, because I saw the UFO. This newspaper is the last copy."

The newspaper article said the UFO landed in the desert for about 20 minutes and then suddenly took off.

We'll never know what might have happened if she had gone to meet them.

Commentary

Borrego Springs is a desert area in San Diego County, California. It is surrounded by Anza-Borrego State Park, the largest of California's State Parks. In 1968, the nighttime skies would have been dark and clear. Later, Borrego Springs village became the first in California to become an "international dark sky" place, and nighttime lighting is kept to a minimum. The area is popular with amateur astronomers.

Not surprisingly, Borrego Springs is a famous UFO hotspot, and numerous sightings of strange lights and unusual aerial activity, including fireball UFOs, have been reported there annually over the years, up to the present.

As Karl Petry notes in "Alien Machine Shop 101," the aliens make it clear that if they want to take us, they will, and there is nothing we can do to prevent it. Yet some of them offer people a choice, such as Norman's mother and Mary Grace O'Meara in "The Alien Examiners." Different aliens, different agendas? We do not know.

Communications from aliens requesting in-person meetings have been documented in the UFO literature. Messages have come in a variety of ways, including Ouija boards and ham radios. The radio used by Maria probably served the same function as a "ghost box" radio device used today for electronic voice phenomena (EVP) messages from spirits and entities. It was, as her son Norman notes, a mediumistic device that enabled mental impressions to form.

In the "space brothers" era following World War II, personal meetings with humanoid aliens were reported. Some of the most famous cases concerned contactees Orfeo Angelucci and George Adamski.

One of Adamski's followers was George Hunt Williamson. In 1952, Williamson, his wife Betty, and their friends Alfred and Betty Bailey began to communicate with aliens via a homemade Ouija board. The aliens suggested switching to ham radio for more efficient communication.

The aliens said they were aboard a spaceship. They dispensed warnings about good and evil alien forces coming to battle on the earth, and made accurate predictions of events that gained the trust of the four people. When the aliens promised to land their ship for a face-to-face meeting, the four were eager to agree.

At the time, they were in the Winslow, Arizona area. The aliens provided a date, time and place. Elated, the Williamsons and Baileys packed up a lunch and set off in two cars. Somehow, they got separated and lost, and missed the appointment – a "chance of a lifetime," lamented Williamson.

The messages from the aliens continued, transmitted via spirit board, ham radio, and telepathy. Williamson became convinced that mass landings were imminent.

Meanwhile, Adamski was getting his own dire warnings of landings and disaster. Williamson and Bailey were among a small group of people that Adamski led into the California desert in November 1952 for a personal meeting with an alien, a Venusian named Orthon. The "meeting," however, consisted of only Adamski walking alone some distance and over a hill out of sight, and then coming back to report on his meeting. The group was cheated out of the experience.

Nonetheless, Williamson backed up Adamski, claiming that a great meeting of telepathic contact had taken place. The incident changed the dynamics of the personal relationships, however, with Adamski withdrawing and becoming more secretive. Williamson and Bailey went their own way.

Perhaps the Williamsons and Baileys – as well as Maria – were lucky that no personal contact took place. Some who have gone off to meet aliens have never returned, despite assurances from the aliens of a round trip.

In 1980, 32-year-old Granger Taylor vanished from his parents' home at Duncan, on Vancouver Island, British Colombia, Canada. Taylor was an ardent UFO enthusiast who built a replica UFO on the property, and fitted it with furniture and a TV. He claimed to be in contact with aliens via dreams.

On November 29, 1980, he left a note for his parents in the barn. It said:

> Dear Mother and Father,
> I have gone away to walk aboard an alien ship, as recurring dreams assured a 42-month interstellar voyage to explore the vast universe, then return.

I am leaving behind all my possessions to you, as I will no longer require the use of any.

Please use the instructions in my will as a guide to help. Love, Granger.

On the back of the note was a map of Waterloo Mountain, 20 miles to the west of the Taylor property.

The Royal Canadian Mounted Police kept up a search for Taylor for about four years. He never returned.

In March 1986, local forestry workers found a blast site near Mount Prevost, not far from Taylor's parents' house. Human bone fragments were found at the scene. Taylor had carried dynamite in his truck to blow up tree stumps. An official coroner's inquest assumed that the remains were those of Taylor, killed when the dynamite somehow exploded.

It's a circumstantial argument, but one that satisfies the authorities. Perhaps Taylor is still out with the aliens.

AN ET VISITOR AT BOWOOD ESTATE
Ron Russell

An entire skywatching team witnesses an ET visitor penetrate a country estate house in England.

In the mid-1990s, I rented a spacious manor house on the Bowood estate in Wiltshire, England and invited Dr. Steven Greer and the CSETI (Center for the Study of Extraterrestrial Intelligence) team to stay there for a week. The house was quite large, with 10 bedrooms, and the windows were inset in stone mullions, a charming feature we don't see in America.

Before the CSETI team arrival, I had a good friend, Paul Vigay, the publisher of the *Enigma* journal and an electronic wiz, scan the house and grounds for any electronic bugs. This was just out of precaution on my part; Steven didn't even know I had done this. Paul found nothing, and I was glad of that.

After Steven and the group of about eight arrived, one of our team leaders, Shari Adamiak, took ill in the evening and was resting in the second-floor master suite bedroom. Steven was by her side and the rest of us decided to do our field work and skywatch on the front lawn about 50 feet from the house. Shari's window was at the second story at the front above where we were sitting.

After 20 minutes several of us noticed a fast-moving bright light in the sky headed our way. We all focused on this light, which appeared out of the ordinary with the speed and altitude it took. It couldn't have been a plane, and we thought it might be a UFO (that's what we were there for after all!), so we watched closely.

The light did not alter speed, it came fast, closer and closer, and we were all astonished to see it go right through the window of Shari's room. The window was composed of stone, metal and glass and no sound was heard. We were astonished to say the least, actually stunned, and began to talk among ourselves comparing what each of us witnessed.

After about 20 minutes Steven came out from the house and said that the most amazing event just happened, an ET spirit being had come right through the window into Shari's room. We all said, "Yes, we all saw it fly right through the window." Steven replied that it had come to help Shari and that we had seen this was very significant. We all said, WOW!

This remains one of the most solid of my paranormal experiences because of all the credible witnesses.

Commentary

Excellent evidence of the same phenomenon is provided independently by multiple witnesses, all of whom interpret it within the context of extraterrestrials. Others might interpret a bright light moving through the sky, and the manifestation of a spirit being in the room of someone who is ill, as an angel. As we have noted elsewhere, one person's angel is another person's ET. Given the background, interests and research focus of the CSETI people, an ET interpretation makes sense and would be expected.

The contact literature has many descriptions of beings labeled ETs who have noncorporeal, spirit forms, and emanate love and healing energy.

Our Biblical ancestors would have known them only as angels, the context appropriate for the worldview in those times.

Whatever the interpretation, the evidence points to something not of this world that happened that night in Wiltshire.

Shari Adamiak passed away on January 20, 1998, after a battle with cancer. She had worked closely with Steven Greer and his CSETI groups for about six years.

HUMAN-ALIEN HYBRIDS ON EARTH
Jacquelin Smith

A psychically gifted woman and animal communicator discusses her relationships with her star family and why she is a hybrid human-extraterrestrial on Earth.

My journey started when my mother was pregnant with me, and she was taken aboard a starship. My soul was present, and I communicated telepathically with the beings while they did a procedure on my mother. I agreed, I volunteered, to be part of a program of being a bridge between what we call star beings and humankind. They injected a cocktail of DNA from seven different star-being races into her womb.

    I don't remember my birth on Earth, but my mother said it was a forced labor birth. I think I had second thoughts about coming here!

    I have always been drawn to UFOs. I have never felt like I "belonged" here. My earliest Earth memory of star beings was when I was still in the crib. One of my first conscious memories was when there was a severe storm – we later found out it was a tornado – and while I was lying in my bed watching the lightning, the star beings came and took me to their starship to comfort me.

I was on the starship off and on a lot from my early childhood, through my teens, and adulthood, receiving many teachings. They taught me about frequencies – that everything has its own frequency. They taught me about harmonics, the frequencies of crystals, color, healing, communicating by telepathy, teleportation, and how to use energy to heal. They taught me how to play with balls of light and orbs and how to create different forms and colors.

They also taught me about my cosmic roots. They had a portal on the craft that would open up like an eye or the aperture of a camera. I would look into it and see into other dimensions and galaxies. I don't recall that they explained how it worked, but I did understand that everything is based on frequency.

Like a movie, I could watch other galaxies, another planet or another being.

The beings were very loving. They had emotions, and I felt nurtured by them. They would laugh at my questions from time to time, because I wanted to know about everything. They had a beautiful laugh, like a bird sound.

I had relaxed and positive experiences with them, and never felt like a victim.

I call them star beings but to me they are simply "beings." These beings were about 5 feet 7 inches tall, humanoid-looking, with black almond-shaped eyes and long thin fingers. They showed me that this appearance was like a suit of shimmering white light that they wore. Underneath their true being was a really beautiful bluish light that was radiant. They said, "This is who we really are. We are appearing to you more humanoid-looking so that you won't be scared."

These beings, who are my star parents, are Tall White Zeta hybrids from a star system close by, Alpha Centauri – they said they came from the future as well as the present.

My first conscious sighting was at 14 years old. I had difficult experiences throughout childhood, and I had been asking for a starship to come and get me because I didn't get along with my parents – but who does at 14? Within a week or two, a ship came in the middle of the day, in a wooded area not far from my house. A huge metallic disk came straight down, so low it was unbelievable, about the height of two houses stacked on top of each other. I could see the portal on the craft. It was silent and made right angle movements in the shape of a cross. I wasn't scared, but then I thought maybe I should rethink calling them in to get me out of here. They took me aboard the starship then and began preparing me to take eggs. They eventually took eggs from me and created hybrid children. They did this a number of times through my teens. Later, they came and put in an implant and then later on took the embryo from me.

I have about 40 hybrid children who are on different spacecrafts and elsewhere. One of them is here on Earth. Am I wild that they harvested my eggs? Part of me had mixed feelings about that, but I have a deeper understanding now. I look at it this way: How wonderful that I could contribute on this evolutionary level and, how exciting to be a part of bridging different cosmic beings. What a great honor and privilege!

Three of the hybrids were created with a man I had known in childhood. When I was 6 to 8 years old, there was a boy I played with in the neighborhood. We had a kinship. I remember him being on the ship as well. We separated, and then 20 years later wound up doing student teaching in the same classroom. I had memories later on of being on a starship where we were together to create hybrid children.

I met some of my hybrid children, which was hard for me and left me feeling very sad. The beings encouraged me to hold them. Again, I had many mixed feelings about this because I never wanted to leave them after visiting them on the ships. One of the children had green eyes like me and it affected me deeply. A few of them had black eyes. Some had thin hair, others had no hair, some had blonde hair like mine. All of them are doing their work and are bridges between various species.

Some of them were not well. When I saw them they were very young. They were created to help their species and other species and to create more connections between Earth and other cosmic species. They are interested in how humans function emotionally. These beings were compassionate loving beings who care about humans and Earth.

There are a lot of star being races who are blending and creating hybrids, in other dimensions as well.

In 1982, I had my first contact with the beings from my original star family, an etheric collective called Quabar. They are pure love and light, and they come from the seventh universe from Earth. They do not have names, but identify themselves by frequencies of energy. At first, I told them to leave me alone, but then a month or so later, I understood what was going on, and was comfortable with it. They are my star family.

I have had many messages and teachings from Quabar. I am a medium and can go into deep trance and let them speak through me, but I usually communicate with them telepathically. They say they are here to assist humanity, and they are encouraging humanity to continue to wake up, evolve and move forward to embrace other beings in the cosmos. In relation to me, they said they would help me in my work to be of benefit to others. They have taught me how to understand "light language." I speak light language from many star-being cultures to help shift the DNA in others and for alignment and healing as well.

My star family is very loving, and they care deeply about humanity – all beings on Earth. They can only intervene so much, as they have what we would call a prime directive. They're doing what they can, but it's up to humanity to evolve.

There are different alliances of star beings, and Quabar is part of an alliance that includes the Mantis beings – I've had a lot of communication with them too, and I am very connected to them. This alliance is part of the Galactic Federation. Quabar introduced me to other beings that I already knew, but had "forgotten" when I came to Earth.

When I communicate with Quabar and other star beings – and I've had experiences with hundreds of different kinds – it creates a strong energetic bridge between humans, them and other cosmic beings. I am one of many here who are part of offering service. All of this opens the collective of humanity, to wake them up and to help them remember their roots and that the truth is we are all cosmic citizens.

I do the same work with the animals – they communicate with me about the many star systems they are from, and why they are on Earth. They show me their essences. They are star beings just as we are.

I teach classes on how to communicate with star beings, animals, plants, trees and all living forms. The plants and trees are star beings as well. I've connected with star beings who are part humanoid and plant. I call them plant-like beings. They resemble our plants and trees, and are on other planets that I visit.

I love sharing this with others. For me, it's a lot of fun and helps them to awaken to who they truly are. I literally live multidimensionally – I'm an interdimensional traveler. I focus on the positive, and offer healing work to people as well as their animal companions.

Many people fear star beings; fear attracts lower frequency beings. We have to move past the fear to attract the higher frequency beings. I had to move past fear myself – initially I was frightened by some of the appearances of the beings. We have to remember that the beings are shapeshifters, and present the way they look for a reason. Some can be quite beautiful, but their intentions are not good while others can appear ugly to us, but are very loving. We have to learn to read their frequencies.

There is a great deal of progress happening in humanity – we are waking up to our star origins. Many of us have star being frequencies operating in our lives, in varying degrees, depending on our soul agreements.

The key message of all these beings is that they all are about love, light and joy. We are all evolving because that's the nature of the multiverse, to continue to grow in various ways.

Quabar has explained that the cosmos is like a spiral that opens and closes. That's the evolutionary process. It's difficult for me to put these frequencies into the limitations of language. They are learning from us and we are learning from them. Some people think star beings are our salvation. I don't think that's true. They are us and we are them. We are all one.

Commentary

Alien-human hybrids on Earth are a part of the contact spectrum that has gained more attention as individuals such as Jacquelin Smith have stepped forward to tell their stories. The hybrids speak of positive experiences and are a counterbalance to the negative abductions that have been published since the 1980s. Negative experiences sell in the media, and so it is no surprise that for several decades the average person might have formed the impression that any alien contact would be traumatic. Certainly, negative experiences do, and continue to, happen, but they do not account for all contact experiences.

Contactee surveys conducted since the start of the 21st century show that many people feel their experiences with aliens are benign to benevolent, and that they are transformed in positive ways as a result. Many speak to onsets of psychic ability and healing ability, a feeling of being somehow "rewired," and an increase in interest in their own spirituality – not religion, but rather spirituality that is independent of religion. Some say they participate in genetics programs for the creation of hybrids, and some, like Jacquelin, say they are hybrids themselves.

Their views of the aliens with whom they are in contact include extraterrestrials, undefined "higher beings," and even future versions of themselves.

The hybridization is held to be part of the ascension process, the evolution of the human soul. Ascension originally referred to the resurrected body of Jesus when he was taken up into heaven. Today it is applied more broadly to the spiritualization of consciousness that will change the body from a physical form to an ethereal "light body," and to the merging of consciousness into the One or All. From the hybrid perspective, alien beings participate in this process as well.

Modern hybrids say they are benefitting both sides, and are well placed to help raise human awareness and improve the frequency of consciousness.

Hybrids who look like, and can function as, ordinary humans surely have an advantage over more obviously alien life forms. The nature of the alien presence on Earth has been speculated upon for many years. Certainly, the Earth seems to have had alien visitors since ancient times, but actual aliens who can live among people is another matter.

One famous – and very controversial – case was Raechel Nadien (an assumed name), the subject of a book titled Raechel's Eyes *(2005) by Helen Littrell and Jean Bilodeaux. According to the story, Raechel was a Zeta Reticulan hybrid who became – with U.S. government approval – an "adopted daughter" for a "Humanization Project." Her human adopted father, Harry, was in the U.S. Air Force in the 1950s and was involved in interactions with aliens from landed and crashed craft. In 1969, he rescued Raechel from a crashed craft. Raechel was later enrolled in a college and became the roommate of Helen's legally blind daughter, "Marisa" (a pseudonym).*

Raechel was quite peculiar, always covered from head to foot in clothing and always wearing black wraparound sunglasses. She ate only a mushy green, spinach-like substance, which she warned Marisa not to touch, or it would make her sick. The food was always delivered to Raechel by Men In Black figures who drove old black cars.

One day in 1972, Helen was visiting her daughter at the rented off-campus apartment she shared with Raechel, and Raechel returned unexpectedly. She tripped and fell into Helen, who was able to touch her spongy, unhuman skin. More startling, Raechel's sunglasses went askew and revealed avocado-green, cat-like, obviously unhuman eyes.

Shortly after that, Raechel left the school, and she and Harry disappeared. Marisa is now deceased.

The new wave of hybrids is out in the open, giving interviews and writing about their star origins. Although some claim to carry "star DNA," no baseline testing has been done to establish the unknown strands.

THE GREAT WHITE BROTHERHOOD
Rosemary Ellen Guiley

A man becomes a healer after dream and spaceship visits from the Great White Brotherhood.

I've met a fair number of spiritual healers over the years, and I always find it interesting to learn how their healing gifts opened to them. The origins differ, but the result is the same – an ability to transfer the vital life force that can have a therapeutic effect, even a miraculous healing.

In 1994, I took a trip to Gulf Breeze, Florida to participate in skywatching for UFOs. Gulf Breeze, located on the Florida panhandle, was at the time a UFO hotspot, gripped in a wave of frequent sightings of lights and craft, and even craft that were seen to enter and emerge from the gulf waters. Steven Greer was there with some of his CSETI (Center for the Study of Extraterrestrial Intelligence) team. Every night, large crowds of skywatchers gathered at various sites for their vigils. I did see strange aerial maneuvers of mystery lights, but had no encounters with craft or alien beings.

During the long nighttime vigils, I got acquainted with some of the other skywatchers. One of them was a man named Todd (a pseudonym), who shared with me his extraordinary experiences with the Great White Brotherhood that resulted in an opening of healing powers.

I asked Todd for a healing session, and he graciously obliged. The next night, he did a laying on of hands. I felt a great deal of heat and a tingling like electricity, both of which are common to touch healing. The session was beneficial, and I felt markedly restored.

He then told me his remarkable story. His healing ability, he said, was facilitated by the Great White Brotherhood, who were giving him teaching and instruction in alternate realities during sleep and by taking him up into their spaceship.

"They are different from angels," he explained. "They are beings of a high dimensional order, who can work in different dimensions, and who are bringers and ministers of spiritual enlightenment. They also work under the direction of God."

He went on, "I believe their purpose is the development of consciousness to higher levels. I sense that they have an extraterrestrial origin, from the Pleiades. But they are not the same as the ETs described in most abduction accounts."

The Great White Brotherhood manifested to him as tall beings wearing white, flowing robes. They were bald, and had no definable facial features. Most of the time, they floated up into his consciousness at night when he closed his eyes and fell into sleep. He also had waking visions of them.

The idea of being a healer had never occurred to Todd prior to these experiences. He was a successful businessman intent on making a lot of money. "But then God stepped in – that wasn't his plan for me," Todd said. "I thought I knew what was best for me, but I didn't. God had other things in mind."

The transformative experiences began on the night of June 7, 1980, when beings in flowing white robes floated into his awareness as he prepared to go to sleep, and invited him to come along with them. Suddenly Todd found himself flying over desert sand. He realized with

The Great White Brotherhood empowers and instructs Todd. Credit: John Weaver.

a start that he was abruptly at the Great Pyramid in Egypt, and he knew that people – or beings – were inside in the apex. No sooner had the thought occurred than he found himself inside the apex, in the company of white-robed beings whose human-like forms were not as dense as physical bodies. He was given to understand, by telepathy, that they were members of the Great White Brotherhood, and they resided in the pyramid's apex. The beings told Todd that he would be given instruction that would make him proficient in certain skills.

About two weeks later, phenomena began manifesting. Todd awakened to a brilliant white light that filled his room, and a roaring sound. Later in the day, while at work, he had a spontaneous out-of-body experience in which he was taken up into light and "cradled in the arms of God." It was so wondrous he did not want to return to his body.

Then began instruction and conditioning. At night, Todd would feel his consciousness go out his window to a spaceship that had physical form, and he would be transported to an otherworldly school where he was instructed. The experiences were interwoven with his dreams. At times, he felt flooded with too much information to process.

The Great White Brotherhood also took Todd in their ship to hover over hydroelectric plants, which somehow were involved in the raising of his own vibrations, his own energy field, so that he could accommodate the tremendous energy that he would use for healing.

Evidence associated with the visitations was witnessed by some of Todd's neighbors, who reported seeing hot, pulsing pink globes of light, 12 to 20 feet in diameter, in his backyard.

The urge to heal by touch began in the same month as his initiation, but it was several years before he allowed himself to use his new ability. Initially, Todd said, he resisted his transformation and argued with God about it, but to no avail. His life turned upside down. To accept what was happening meant turning away from everything he had worked toward on the material plane.

In 1984, he sold his business and went to Sedona, Arizona, a place to which he felt intuitively drawn, and which calls thousands of spiritual pilgrims every year because of the "vortex energy" there. He stayed two years, integrating his experiences, and then returned to Gulf Breeze.

Early on, Todd turned to the Bible to better understand what he was being called to do. "That's the only way I can find myself," he said. He cited the books of Daniel, Isaiah and Ezekiel as being of particular help to him, as well as the New Testament, which concerns spiritual awareness and expansion.

Todd's interdimensional experiences continued to the time I met him, 14 years later. By then, the nightly schooling has largely given way to waking visions, remote viewing, clairvoyant viewing into the fourth and fifth dimensions, Christ-inspired direct voice mediumship, direct clairaudient messages from the voice of God, and more. One of his most dramatic waking visions occurred on the morning of December 13, 1991, when hearts floated through Todd's ceiling and down to the floor, growing in size as they descended. His interpretation of the vision was that he was being given a sign of God's tremendous love.

Todd continued his intense study of the Bible. Healing, he said, "is not something I do alone, or to glorify myself. I am here to witness to the Holy Spirit. I give all the glory to Jesus and to God. To me, the Holy Spirit is alive, and through me, the Holy Spirit does loving things to others. I've learned that God is not law, but love."

In giving a healing, Todd centered himself and prayed to God for healing, loving energy to flow down from the Christ level through him and go where it would do the most good. He sometimes felt himself vibrating like a high-voltage wire, with alternating currents moving up and down his hands, arms and shoulders. "It's an energy that has a high frequency," he told me. "I can feel it leaving my body, and pulsating in my body when it's at a high level."

He also felt pulses of light emanating from his forehead, where the third eye is located. He was told by some people that they could see light emanating from his eyes.

Todd viewed his own experiences as part of a greater whole, an expansion of consciousness awakening in many other people. His vision of the hearts descending from the ceiling was a sign to him also that humankind is about to be "quantum-leaped" in consciousness. "We're going to have a new way of being," he said. "I don't know exactly when that is going to take place. From the visions I've seen, it's going to be soon."

His transformation, he said, was part of a prelude to a great mass healing of consciousness. "Some of us are introduced to higher levels of consciousness early," he said, "so that when the rest are introduced, they can help others deal with it, especially psychologically."

I asked Todd if he thought Earth changes were part of the change in consciousness. "I think so," he answered, "because the Earth is full of energy, and surely it will change as our energy changes."

He did not foresee cataclysms and tribulation. "I've not seen doom and gloom," he said, referring to his visions. "The worst I've seen is something not being healed. This is in the Scripture. It's in John in the New Testament that not everyone is going to be healed."

Todd said his own goal was striving for perfection. He had learned from his experiences that when energy is given out to others, it is replaced by an even higher and better energy.

I stayed in touch with Todd for a few years, and then the tides of change interrupted the connection. I made no more trips to Gulf Breeze. I do not know how long he stayed with his healing, or where his path took him. His experiences and visions were similar to others I have encountered, raising questions about the higher purpose of our encounters with alien beings, spirits and entities.

Commentary

The Great White Brotherhood is described as a society of human saints and ascended masters, angels and "cosmic beings" who work to disseminate spiritual knowledge and skills to selected individuals. They wear flowing white robes; hence their name. The co-founder of Theosophy, Helena P. Blavatsky, was the first to talk about the Great White Brotherhood, and said she received messages from them. Subsequently others also have said they were in contact with the brotherhood, among them Alice Bailey, noted Theosophist; Guy Ballard, the founder of the I AM movement; Aleister Crowley, the infamous occultist; and Elizabeth Clare Prophet.

Some say the Brotherhood can be identified in the Bible. Revelation 7:9 describes "...a great multitude that no one could count, from every nation, tribe, people and language, standing before the throne and before the Lamb. They were wearing white robes and were holding palm branches in their hands."

Anyone can have experiences with the Great White Brotherhood, and their impressions and interpretations have some variance. For Todd, the brotherhood was perceived more as a group of cosmic beings who were different from angels and ETs. Because of his background, he also interpreted the beings and his experiences from a religious point of view.

His association of the Brotherhood with the Pleiades is unusual, but neither right nor wrong in general; rather, it was right for him. In most encounters, the aliens do not state where they are from. However, when they do, the Pleiades is the most frequently mentioned place. For several decades, the Pleiadians have been channeled as sources of cosmic wisdom.

Many people who have or develop extraordinary healing ability attribute their gift to the intervention of otherworldly figures of many kinds. They often integrate their experiences within the context of religion or spiritual faith.

Like Todd, they describe powerful energy moving through them and a marked change in their consciousness and even physical form.

In Todd's experiences, the spaceships and the hydroelectrical power are interesting factors. There are many cases on record of UFOs and craft being observed hovering near hydroelectrical and nuclear power plants, and the speculation is that they may be drawing energy from them.

Many contact experiences (including ET abductions) have involved perceptions of "the world to come" and "Earth changes." Almost all of them address mass shifts in consciousness to a higher, more spiritual level, and even physical transformations to less dense "light bodies." Some see apocalyptic cataclysms and destruction; others see a more gradual and less traumatic shift. Many see ETs and cosmic beings playing a significant role in this transformation.

Todd's words still ring true years later. Research of alien contact experiences indicates that contact with "nonhuman intelligent beings" seems to be on the increase, and that many of these experiences are positive, not negative. Experiencers today echo the experiences and views of Todd and others in the past. Many experiencers say that their contact is followed by kundalini-like changes that include the onset of healing energy and "high frequency" energy coursing through the body, psychic powers (especially precognition and telepathy), a greater and more spiritual connection to "Everything That Is," and cosmic-consciousness types of experiences which, in the past, would be found only in the literature of saints and mystics.

HIGH STRANGENESS

THE SCORPION PORTAL
Ron Russell

A man experiences an apparent time warp when he walks out of a crop circle formation in England at night.

In the summer of 1994, I went to southern England to study the crop circles. The crop formations are intentional embossments in the fields of wheat or other grains and cereal crops. The embossments occur at night and then there's the formation of circles, boxes, lines, whatever, in the fields the next morning.

I worked with the Center for Crop Circle Studies (CCCS) in England on a number of studies on the effects on people who visited crop circles. Our exit polls of people randomly visiting these formations were that 20 percent of them seemed to have ecstatic experiences of heightened frequency; 20 percent seemed to have negative experiences; and the rest were neutral and did not report any kind of alteration in their moods.

We believed at the time that many of these formations were not man-made, although some of them certainly were. But even the man-made ones, if they were made in certain powerful locations with the right intent, had significant effects on people who went into them.

I was flying in a Cessna on August 13, 1994 with fellow crop circle researcher and pilot Busty Taylor over the Avebury area. I was photographing the formations that already existed, and in the flight in the early afternoon we found a formation that wasn't there the day before. Busty had flown there every day taking pictures with various people who wanted aerial photographs. On that day, he said, "My God, that wasn't there before!"

This was right behind a little hamlet known as Avebury Trusloe in the Wiltshire District in southwest England, north of Stonehenge. Both Busty and I began snapping away, taking photographs. Then we flew back to the airport.

At my earliest opportunity that evening, I went into the circle myself to see what I could feel from that formation.

I entered the formation about 11 o'clock at night with a friend of mine from California, John. He had been in England for several years. We had no trouble finding the formation and parked the car. We entered the formation going through a wire fence and walking a short distance.

The formation was nearly 260 feet in diameter – a big ring with 13 circles of diminishing size displayed within the ring, and with a little crescent tail.

We had had six or seven formations called *"scorpions"* that year. That appellation may have been a distortion, but they seemed to be insect-like in nature. There were many circles laid out in a slight curve with a little crescent tail. We thought that this one looked like an embryonic scorpion – a nested scorpion – within the larger circle. That, I believe was the name that the CCCS was going to attach to it.

When we went into this formation, John sat down to meditate. I took my 35-mm Fuji pocket camera to make quick flash records of the circular patterns within the larger circle. I wanted to record the formation before people got to it and messed it up. I thought we were the first people into this formation, which was quite well hidden and couldn't be easily seen from the road. Since it had just appeared late the night before, it was only one day old by the time we visited it and I didn't want to lose the pristine evidence.

Then I ran out of film. I thought I'd better hurry and get some more film, fearing that if I didn't complete taking photos, the formation would soon be ruined, and any important clues lost. John was still doing his meditation, so I headed back to the car to fetch more film.

I walked down the same tram lines that we entered before. A tram line is the line in the field where the tractor drives to fertilize or put fungicide on the crops. It is a little track that goes through the field, so the tractor can move about without crushing the crop. They're the width of a tractor and they're usually spaced about 40 or 60 feet apart.

I walked for 15 or 20 minutes down the tram line, thinking to myself that something was a little odd – I wasn't reaching the car! I made the appropriate turn on a crossing tram line, and I still didn't reach the car. So, I continued walking for another 10 or 15 minutes.

Now, I became a little concerned that I was perhaps lost, although I couldn't rationally figure out how I could be lost in such a small field at night, especially when I knew my way around these formations. I did think that maybe something strange was happening, but I didn't want to prejudge it, and so, I just kept walking down the tram line.

But the tram line got narrower and narrower, which was odd, because tram lines don't narrow! They just stop at the point where a tractor enters.

I was walking down this one tram line when it diminished, became smaller and narrower until, finally, there was no more tram line. I couldn't understand how that could happen.

Now I was walking through the virgin crop, which I don't like to do. I was very careful. I don't like to crush somebody else's property, and I was in this field without permission late at night. I thought by now it was probably after midnight.

I felt by my internal sense of time that about 30 or so minutes had passed since I had left John meditating in the circle. And that amount of time would be okay, in and of itself, but I was a little apprehensive about getting back late: it would take me another 30 minutes or so, and that would be an elapsed time of about an hour, which would be strange and maybe upsetting to John.

However, as I was debating what to do, I saw a village ahead of me, a little group of huts through the brush and trees at the edge of the field. I was finally coming to the edge of the field. I could see fire – little bonfires, cooking fires. I could hear voices. I could smell meat cooking. I saw a little cluster of thatched cottages that were small and primitive. I heard the voices of children and dogs. I noticed that the air was thick. I got to within 20 yards of this little hamlet and I thought to myself that I must be approaching the 15th century or some part of the Middle Ages! I thought, *How could this be? This village is not around here that I know of – and I know the area fairly well.*

I thought I might have slipped through a time doorway or portal of some kind.

I was not frightened, oddly enough; rather, I was elated! I thought, *What a fantastic opportunity this is! I've got a camera!* But suddenly it dawned on me that I was out of film, and I had been on my way to get more film, and now, here I was with a camera that was useless to record anything significant.

Then a scary thought occurred to me, *My God, this could be trouble! If this IS the 15th century or whatever, and I've got a camera and modern clothing and a modern accent to my speech, I could be looked on as a devil or threat and burned at the stake in very short order!*

I wasn't especially fearful of that, but, nevertheless, I was a bit apprehensive. Who wouldn't be? It began to dredge up memories, old ancient memories, that I didn't want to repeat traumatic experiences, so I thought to myself, *Well, this is the way to solve it: I'll go back, and I'll get John, and I'll bring him into this. Somehow, we'll solve this problem together.*

I carefully turned around, retraced my steps, took the appropriate turns, walked for quite a long time, maybe 25 or 30 minutes, and got back just the way I had come. I got back into the formation, and there, sure enough, was John standing there.

I said, "John, I'm really sorry I've been gone so long. I got lost."

And he replied, "Gone? We've only been here 10 minutes!"
I said, "Well, John, I'm certain I've been gone an hour! I don't have a watch on, but I definitely feel that a huge amount of time has passed."

He said, "No, no. We've only been here a few minutes! And I just had a very short meditation." He added, "What are you up to?"

I just couldn't believe it!

I told him, "Well, I think I found a doorway through time, and I was only 20 yards from the 15th century. I'd like you to come back with me, if you will."

He said, "Oh, wow! Let's go!"

We retraced our steps. I took the same path that I had taken before, and within just about three minutes, what the hell – we were back at the car! I said, "This is impossible. The car's not here. I just went down this pathway, and there was no car!"

John said, "Well, look Ron, maybe we should come back and look at this in the morning. It's getting pretty late. We don't want to make a lot of noise out here."

I said, "Okay. Crack of dawn we'll come back, and I'll walk the perimeter of this field, and you will see where the village is."

We did that at 6:30 the next morning. I took more photos in the formation. I walked around the perimeter of the field, which was small, and there was no village at all, and there was no evidence to that effect. It was as if it never had been! "Where'd it go?"

This still is a mystery to me, and I do tend to trust my own experiences: they don't often deceive me! I truly don't think I was deceived in this experience. I think it did happen, I did go through a doorway, or portal, or something, but I just wasn't able to repeat it.

Possibly the crop circle had something to do with it. Maybe the energy in that location engendered this kind of experience. I talked with people in the community about this in a guarded way the next day.

People said, "Oh my, people are disappearing all the time around here. We know so and so, and she didn't come back for three weeks! She said she went into an alternate world."

Many people confirmed there were, indeed, these doorways. But when I asked for specific locations, they would be very vague about it, as if it were a kind of a prosaic thing to them, and they didn't care to get involved in it any further.

I heard that there were people who disappeared and never came back. I also heard a rumor that the British military had fenced off certain areas in Britain around some sacred sites, where people were alleged to have disappeared and never returned. Unlike me, maybe they did go through time portals, but didn't stop and turn around – maybe they went all the way and never came back!

This may be related to the fairy legends, in which people go off with fairies, or find entrances to the fairy realm, and disappear. I think that the veil that separates our material reality from another parallel reality is very thin and perhaps is torn in parts of England as well as in other sacred parts of the world.

In hindsight, I would have taken my coat off, dropped my camera, and made myself a little trail that I could mark in a subtle way, that I would know was my trail. I would then continue into the village and at least make a tentative encounter. It's possible that I would not have encountered fear from the residents or some rigid belief system, which would want to destroy me for being different. But even if I did come across some danger, I think I could quickly run back along the escape route. I felt I lost a real opportunity there.

Many researchers have had many paranormal experiences in this area and in the circles.

We did some work with Dr. Joachim Koch and the dowser Hans Jurgen Kyborg from Germany, who had discovered energy grid patterns through dowsing, and they found many formations with grid patterns superimposed on them. They felt "scanned" in some formations as if some *one* or some *thing* took notice of them somehow. They told me that there was a good such "pattern" on the top of Windmill Hill, in particular.

So, I went to Windmill Hill and I, myself, felt this scanning sensation. I did a meditation and when I came out of the meditation I felt that my reality had changed in some way, as if there was something kinder and gentler about the universe that I now inhabited than the one that I left only 30 minutes before.

The stone circle disappearance

I heard of a person who disappeared in a sacred stone circle.

A friend of mine from Wales went with a group of people to Avebury to a stone circle. One of the group of about 20 people got in the center of that circle. The others held hands around the outside to bless and heal her, and they began to move in a counter-clockwise direction during their meditation, chanting, and so forth. Suddenly she vanished out of the circle apparently into thin air. Nobody could figure out what happened, and for 30 minutes they milled about and wondered what to do.

Suddenly, somebody came up with the idea, "Well, maybe we ought to form our circle again and do the same thing but maybe this time rotate in the opposite direction."

That's exactly what they did. And bingo – she appeared instantaneously in the center of the circle, roundly cursing out her friends for "abandoning" her to a transparent cylinder that she couldn't get out of. She said she was hammering on the walls and screaming at them. She said she could see them, but they couldn't see her!

Commentary

"Crop circle effects" are reported by many people who enter formations, as Ron noted. They can be positive or negative. Positive effects include euphoria, light-headedness, drowsiness, expansion, a sense of cosmic connection, loss of time, and even mystical rapture. Negative effects include headaches and body pains, nausea, unease, and foreboding. Some people feel nothing unusual.

Opinions have been sharply divided over the years among crop circle researchers and enthusiasts as to whether human-made formations can produce such effects. They can, and so crop circle effects are not a marker of human versus alien/unknown origin explanations. Nor are all formations uniform in effects.

We can only speculate why effects happen. Some are self-induced by individuals who have preconceived expectations. Some may be due to the land, which may have certain magnetic anomalies that are capable of having physical and psychological effects on people. Magnetic anomalies and their effects upon people have been documented in non-crop circle locations.

Ron observes that the land may have some special characteristics, given the history cited by the locals. Such anomalies may stretch back in history, to times when fairy lore was strong.

Some crop circle effects may be created in part by the actual making of the formation, regardless of maker. When humans make something by hand, they imbue energy, emotion and intention into their creation. Perhaps these forces mix with the natural energies of the land, and then in turn with the people who enter formations. Depending on their sensitivity, effects vary.

In Ron's case, he had no expectations, certainly none of a time slip.

If alien forces are responsible for some formations, then they may imbue an energy as well. We also have to consider whether people, unconsciously or deliberately, work in concert with spiritual or alien energy to create crop circles. Many individuals and groups have experimented with "meditating" circles into formation. Do they link up to aliens, earth spirits or other beings? Do they make a telepathic connection with human circle makers who are then "inspired"? We do not know where the boundaries are, or if boundaries exist at all.

Whoever or whatever made the scorpion formation, it perhaps magnified a charged energy that produced a time slip for Ron, an effect that was verified by others as having happened in the same area before.

The stone circle disappearance is an odd case. By walking counter-clockwise, the group was walking "widdershins," or against the sun, which in the folklore of witchcraft and magic is used to cast "undoing" spells. Counter-clockwise, or "deosil," is a manifesting energy. Here again this event may have been the result of a combination of energetic forces: land, stone circle, people.

ESCAPADE AT AREA 51
Michael Brein

Three men share a rollicking adventure trying to get close to one of America's most top secret air bases.

The place: Area 51, located at Groom Lake, a salt flat 20 miles south of the tiny town of Rachel, Nevada. Area 51 is a highly-classified detachment of Edwards Air Force Base. According to UFO rumors and conspiracy theories, the black projects at Area 51 have included the storage of recovered alien spacecraft, including the alleged crashed craft from Roswell, New Mexico in 1947; the reverse engineering of alien craft; storage of live and dead aliens; and the development of time travel and teleportation technologies. At the time of this adventure in 1994, it was possible to drive up to the perimeter of Area 51 – if one knew what one was doing.

The players: Ufologist Michael Brein, crop circle researcher George Wingfield, and Glenn Campbell, ufologist and civilian expert on Area 51.

Let's define "trouble" as setting out for America's most top secret airbase, namely, "Area 51," with the aim of seeing what's going on there.

All well and good, except that when traveling with George Wingfield, watch out! There's sure to be trouble a-h-e-a-d!

Travels with George

I can't begin to tell you how I got myself into this mini-adventure-morass, but it all began with my picking up my English friend, George Wingfield, at a weeklong UFO conference just outside Las Vegas, which he was attending.

The plan was for me to collect him there and drive up north through Nevada, stopping to garner a view of the world-renowned airbase, Area 51, and to see what kind of trouble we could get ourselves into. Then, I was to deposit him in the Bay Area for his departure home.

To get to Rachel from Las Vegas, we traveled up the *Extraterrestrial Highway*, renamed to promote tourism to the area. In Rachel, we rented rooms in a small trailer court that was part of the famous Little A'le'Inn, a tavern known for its collection of UFO lore. It was all decked out with aliens in every shape and form (plastic or rubber – not the real deal), along with all sorts of other UFO paraphernalia and memorabilia.

The Inn, along with the secret base, was a major mecca for the more adventurous UFO buffs, who did skywatching at night in hopes of catching odd sights, and who also ventured out to the boundary of Area 51. Those who were lucky and ballsy enough would get a peek at the facility from a vantage point on public Bureau of Land Management (BLM) land.

Signs posted at the end of the public road forbade trespassing as well as even taking photos of the sign, on pain of death, *literally!* The threats were very specific and left no room for deliberation!

You can understand why George and I were lured by the specter of the excitement, adventure, and uncertainty involved in going to Area 51. Whether you believe in the reality of UFOs; whether you think they are here or not; you might imagine that the thrill of checking all this out was a powerful magnet for throngs of flying saucer curiosity-seekers who have made the pilgrimage to Area 51. It certainly was for us.

In Rachel, we looked up the self-styled Area 51 expert, Glenn Campbell, at his trailer home. At the time, he was publishing his magazine, *The Groom Lake Desert Rat*, on the Internet, and it was from this that we had learned of his exploits.

Glenn had discovered a mountain ridge near Tikaboo Valley from which it was possible to see down into the Groom Lake base from a distance of 12 miles, and observe with telescopes and binoculars some of the activities going on there. He called this viewpoint "Freedom Ridge." It was on BLM public land just outside the perimeter of Area 51. You could be intimidated there, but you could not be arrested for going there.

More balls than brains?

Glenn offered to take us across the desert through Tikaboo Valley to Freedom Ridge, and so we set out in his Jeep Cherokee. Despite the fact that it was public land, the Area 51 guards – who he called the "Cammo Dudes" – kept a watchful eye out for intruders and discouraged those who came too close to the back entrance to the huge base.

They could often be seen sitting in their vehicles, scanning the dirt roads and the sagebrush with binoculars for any unwanted intruders. These guys were armed and meant business, and the warning notices near the perimeter markers made it quite clear that deadly force would be used if necessary.

Glenn briefed us about what we needed to do to reach Freedom Ridge without being intercepted by the Cammo Dudes. The approach was monitored with special electronic sensors that were concealed in places along the road in the sagebrush. A passing vehicle would trigger such a hidden sensor and cause it to send a radio signal, which could then be picked up at the base.

George asked, "How the hell are we going to get past these and not set off an alarm every time we drive close to one?"

Glenn grinned and said that he had it all worked out. He took out a map that he created of Tikaboo Valley showing the positions of the sensors, which he had discovered on his previous sorties. He also produced a detector meter, which could pick up the signals of the frequency used by these Area 51 alarms.

Mr. "Good Citizen"

Comforted by his assurances, George sat with this sensor detector box on his lap, and we set off. I was serving as a "watchful eye."

Glenn chuckled, "You'll soon see if we trigger a sensor, as the needle on the dial will jump up to that frequency, and there will be no mistaking if that happens!" He laughed.

Of course, this was to be a worst-case scenario, and hopefully an unlikely one. It was not comforting in the least to hear him saying this. *What are we getting ourselves into,* I wondered?

We drove on without speaking through the public BLM desert area. When Glenn knew there was a sensor coming up, he would stop the Jeep and get out. He'd then walk forward, looking in the sagebrush for the device, which consisted of a sensor head and a cable about 15 feet long connected to a battery box, on top of which was a small vertical aerial that sent out the alarm signal.

When he found a sensor close to the dirt road, he traced the cable back into the scrub to find the battery box. He unscrewed the aerial and returned to the Jeep with a confident smile on his face. Then, he drove on about 30 yards beyond where the device was located.

Then he went back on foot and reattached the aerial, thus leaving the U.S. Government property undamaged and exactly as he found it. So far, so good. Glenn certainly did have brains! But did he have more balls than brains? Only time would tell.

When he had successfully dealt with three of these devices shown on his map, we heaved a sigh of relief and drove on to Freedom Ridge.

Unfortunately, our relief was somewhat premature. Suddenly and silently, the needle on the detector in front of George leaped to a frequency – the alarm frequency!

"We've blown it. We've *really* blown it!" George gasped. "There must be a new device which isn't on your map!"

Sure enough, the alarm signal had been transmitted, and some 13 miles away at the secret base, they were now very much aware that intruders were approaching the perimeter. None of us felt very good at that moment! Was all hell going to break loose? Would George (a U.K. citizen) be permanently banned from ever visiting his beloved America again?

A Black Hawk helicopter confronts the intruders. Credit: John Weaver.

Scared the Bejeezus out of Us!

Within a few minutes, we heard the *whomp, whomp, whomp* of a powerful helicopter flying up the valley towards us. It flew in a zigzag pattern obviously looking for the intruding vehicle.

As it drew closer, we saw it was a large Black Hawk helicopter. Fixed underneath its nose there was what appeared to be a long, heavy "machine gun." I wondered if that was meant for us?

We had only seconds to hide, and it was obvious that we had no possible way of hiding the Jeep. All three of us leaped from the vehicle and ran to hide behind nearby rocks. The Black Hawk flew towards us at a level of no more than 20 feet off the ground. So close was it that sand and grit were blasted up at us by the down draught of its rotors. It roared above us and then turned and came back at us again.

Through an open hatch in its side, I could see two men with a large video camera filming us. The large "machine gun" appeared to be pointing straight at us, and the rocks gave us very little cover. I felt like we were in a James Bond movie, except that James Bond always managed to escape and prevail. But would we be able to claim the same?

After a third low pass at us, the helicopter flew away, back to the secret base at Area 51. The terror of the moment had passed, and we beat a hasty retreat in case the Cammo Dudes in their SUVs now came after us.

This sandblasting technique by the Black Hawk apparently had been used before to discourage other visitors. None of us had been shot, and I later discovered that the "machine gun" was an inflight-refueling probe.

Not long afterward, George did reach Freedom Ridge with Glenn in his Jeep, but this time without me. Frankly, I had had enough. From the top of the ridge, he watched a large airplane, which he could not identify, land at the base and several other smaller planes land there as well.

For about one year longer, it was possible for people to go there to Freedom Ridge and sometimes watch secret aircraft take off or land. In 1995, the government suddenly withdrew access to an additional several thousand acres of BLM land, which included Freedom Ridge, and blocked off the road that led there with an artificial rockslide.

The Black Hawk helicopters still patrol the outskirts of Area 51, but the sandblasting of intruders is now an extremely rare occurrence.

Now, the perimeters around the base are no longer the domain of the odd mix of UFO characters, curious onlookers, and, no doubt, foreign spies. The secrets of Area 51 are still safe.

I'll never forget the look of fear on George's face, which probably reflected mine as well.

George continued his regular visits to America. Our convictions remained strong in thinking that UFOs are real, whether or not there is any connection between them and the secret base.

Will the visitors ever cease traversing the Extraterrestrial Highway in the hope of seeing something in the skies over Area 51?

Commentary

With the tightening of security measures, Area 51 no longer offers a relatively easy thrill for UFO buffs. The forbidden points are not well marked, or marked at all, and trespassers can find themselves arrested and their equipment confiscated. They may be fined as well.

The Little A'le'Inn continues to draw UFO buffs and curious tourists. The inn opened around 1989 by owners Joe (now deceased) and Pat Travis. In 1991 they held a contest for a more exciting name than the Rachel Bar and Grill, and changed the name to The Little A'le'Inn.

Beliefs persist about the secret alien/UFO activities at Area 51. The rumors came to widespread public attention in 1989 when Bob Lazar claimed to have worked on reverse engineering of alien technology at S-4, a site near Area 51. Lazar remains a controversial figure.

Glenn Campbell became a media celebrity with his knowledge and exploits of Area 51. In the early 2000s, he withdrew from the public eye for a few years, but returned in 2009. He has worked as a media consultant, and is an author and an avid traveler. As of 2017, he was still traveling with no fixed residence.

MISSING TIME AND MISSING EXITS
Anonymous

A man experiences missing time and a strange absence of exits along a normally busy highway while is he tracked by a mystery light.

Have you ever had a mystical experience while traveling? I did. I was driving in my van by myself through southern Utah one night, coming back from an art festival. I saw a light, which seemed to be moving right along with the van as if pacing it. I felt as if it was looking at me. I don't know if it was a UFO or what, but I thought it was unidentified, for sure. It was very peculiar. So, I thought I would get very quiet and try to communicate with it, and quell my formative mind, for a minute. I was then in a meditative state while I was driving – kind of an altered state. Although I tried to ignore the light, the witness in me didn't stop paying attention to it.

Strangely enough, I noticed there were no exits along the freeway. I was going and going and going, and according to my car clock, I was traveling for about 30 minutes with no freeway exits at all coming into view. You know, there's not 30 minutes without any exits that I know of off any freeway. No exits! When I finally did come to an exit, the clock in my car displayed the wrong time. I've never been able to figure that one out. I don't know what that was about. I had to reset my clock. Although I had no watch with me, I felt I'd had a time shift.

I pulled off the exit to gas up. Another peculiar problem was that I apparently hadn't used up any gas during those 30 minutes. The needle on the gauge hadn't moved at all. I thought that was strange.

Commentary

The mystery light seems to pace the driver's van, which is characteristic of other UFO experiences. Such encounters involve isolated stretches of road at night. Lights that pace cars sometimes materialize into craft, forcing drivers to halt. Missing time is often involved.

In this case, the driver is not forced to stop, but rather to continue, apparently for an extraordinary amount of time without the appearance of exits.

In similar cases, individuals have discovered – usually with the help of hypnosis – that something much more took place, such as an abduction. Did the driver's attempt at communication have an influence on what transpired?

Unfortunately, we do not have the exact highway to check exit distances, nor do we know if the driver was traversing east-west or north-south. The I-70, which runs through central Utah east-west, has a stretch of 106 miles without an exit, between Salina and Green River.

Missing time occurs on roads without UFOs, or at least the conscious recall of them. In West Virginia, there is a stretch of Route 55 near the haunted Seneca Rocks where drivers experience missing time and high strangeness. In one case documented by Rosemary in her book The Big Book of West Virginia Ghost Stories *(2014), a truck driver well familiar with Route 55 suddenly noticed that he had been driving for an extraordinary amount of time – more than three hours for what should have been a 30-minute trip. He consulted a map and discovered that he had gotten onto a different road, but without ever exiting Route 55. In his course correction, things still were not right. The road was unusually smooth and exceptionally narrow, with no center line. There were no other vehicles on the road, nor were there any utility poles, road signs or mailboxes – in fact, there were no signs of life, not even wildlife. Everything was unusually still. Suddenly, and as abruptly as the weird experience started, he found himself back in familiar surroundings and reached his destination. He learned that other truck drivers had had similar experiences in the area. He attempted to retrace his journey, and could not.*

Perhaps these experiences are part of portal openings, or "in-between" places in realities. In the case of the Utah driver, the appearance of the tracking UFO may have been a factor in the opening of an "Oz reality."

A "PHREAKING" MAN IN BLACK
Joey Madia

A man and his daughter meet a possible Man In Black in Mothman territory, and high strangeness follows.

An interesting experience happened to my daughter Jolie and I on the way back to North Carolina from Point Pleasant, West Virginia, home of the Mothman, where we had done some paranormal investigating. We might have had an encounter with a Man In Black.

Mothman was a winged humanoid that was part of a wave of paranormal activity from 1966-67 that included UFO lights and craft, aliens, Men In Black, prophecies, and other high strangeness. The star of the show was "Mothman," a dark, winged humanoid with red eyes, which flew around and terrified people. The phenomena ranged over a wide region of the mid-Ohio River Valley, with Point Pleasant being the epicenter.

Our experience happened on July 20, 2015. We had entered Virginia, and a big black moth flew into our car grill. About 10 minutes later, we came upon a Geo Metro hatchback painted a dull black. I remarked to Jolie that I was fascinated because I didn't think any of those cars were still on the road. I was riveted for some unexplainable reason, so much so that she remarked how weird my interest in the car was.

The Metro had a white piece of paper with a black 8 on the dashboard reflecting in the windshield. This was interesting because we had had discussions with a friend a day before our trip that involved the infinity symbol, which looks like an 8 on its side. And, a member of our investigation team in Point Pleasant had heard us talking about the number 8 in the Mothman Museum, and said an upside down 8 is also an 8.

The driver of the Metro was bald, with big dark sunglasses, and was using what looked like an electric razor – but the size of a brick – on his face as he drove. We entered a tunnel just behind him. He immediately shot forward at a very high rate of speed and disappeared well ahead of us. I looked down and I was going 85. So, that Metro was going at least 100 mph.

About an hour later we came upon a black van with an infinity symbol in the back window.

To add to the mystery, just the day before this encounter, our team had been at the Harris Steakhouse in Point Pleasant (the "Mothman Diner" hangout for investigators), where we had a long discussion about MIBs that had been photographed with powerful people. We talked about a 1961 photograph linked to the "Tall Whites" (or "Nordic") ET conspiracy theory that shows President John F. Kennedy and General Curtis LeMay with a tall man in black wearing sunglasses, standing behind them. He and other Tall Whites were rumored to be MIBs who were seen at the White House. Other photos showed Val Valiant Thor, an alleged alien from Venus, who made appearances at the Pentagon for several years in the 1950s and supposedly met with President Dwight D. Eisenhower. And one of the famous MIB photos showed a mysterious black box about the size of a brick.

Three months later, on October 26, I was taking some garbage to the dumpster behind my wife's new holistic healing studio and I "found" a plastic tag in the middle of the parking lot. It was the exact font and white on black from the Number 8 on the "MIB" car that Jolie and I saw in July.

A "Phreaking" Man In Black

I had been doing research that morning about the "phreaking boxes" of the 1960s that college kids once used to make illegal phone calls, for a fiction series I was writing, and they reminded me of the brick-sized "razor" the possible MIB in the car was holding.

Commentary

Encounters with Men In Black, like other "high strangeness" associated with UFOs and related phenomena, often have incongruous elements that make no sense, and involve odd synchronicities that also make no sense.

Having spent time in an area famous for intense UFO and mysterious creature activity, Joey and Jolie then are subjected to high strangeness "fallout" with the MIB in a black car, the number 8 and a black brick-sized device or box.

John A. Keel, the primary researcher of the Mothman wave, once observed that these kinds of phenomena seemed to be deliberately orchestrated by some crafty, Trickster-like intelligence to flummox investigators. When researchers focus their attention and energy on UFOs, for example, or mysterious creatures or MIB, it seems to register on the radar of this intelligence, and it responds.

During the 13-month Mothman wave, Keel documented MIB encounters of equal craziness, numerous reports of mystery lights in the sky, and encounters with craft and aliens, plus much more. The Point Pleasant area is still rife with the unexplained today, although Mothman itself is largely absent.

The phreaking boxes, now obsolete, once were electronic devices that could interface directly with a telephone line and manipulate or disrupt it. The most well-known were black in color; they tricked switching equipment into believing a call had not been answered, resulting in free incoming long-distance calls.

Those who encounter MIBs often say there is something old-fashioned or out of place about them, such as outdated clothing, old cars, and so on – all in black. Geo Metro cars were manufactured from 1989 to 2001, and it was the first generation that was done as a hatchback.

Perhaps with his black box, this MIB was disrupting someone's communication, somewhere in some time.

MEN IN BLACK AT THE LIBRARY
Joey and Tonya Madia

Two mysterious Men In Black lurk about a haunted library in North Carolina.

We started leading paranormal investigations at The Webb Memorial Library & Civic Center in Morehead City, North Carolina, in 2016. The library is famous for being haunted, and UFO activity has been reported in the area as well; we believe there is a connection. We have encountered human spirits, shadow people, black mists, shapeshifters, and even a round, hairy being we have identified as an "interdimensional." Some of these presences are there all the time, and some seem to come and go, as though they are passing through from somewhere. When people notice them, it is usually psychically, such as through clairvoyance or mental and physical impressions. Tonya is mediumistic and can "see" them.

On Memorial Day weekend 2017, we encountered something else entirely unexpected – what can best be described as classic "Men In Black." Most people know about MIBs through the popular films with

Will Smith and Tommy Lee Jones. As fantastic as those films are, they do get some elements right.

MIBs usually manifest in relation to UFOs. Dressed all in black, they show up when someone has seen a UFO or extraterrestrial/interdimensional being – especially if they plan to talk about what they have seen. The MIBs look and act in strange ways, as though they are not entirely in this reality. In fact, they can abruptly vanish, and sometimes they are seen floating rather than walking. They threaten witnesses not to talk about their experiences.

On May 25, 2017, we were conducting our investigation in an upstairs room called the Cannon Room. We use a variety of equipment, including devices to capture EVPs, or Electronic Voice Phenomena. Sometimes we are able to carry on short real-time conversations with some of the resident spirits.

Suddenly our EVP equipment started to jam up, as though it was malfunctioning. Two male figures looking like dark-suited government-types manifested, sitting in chairs by the back bookshelves. The chairs were next to each other with a small table in between.

Tonya was the only person in the group of eight investigators who could see the figures clairvoyantly. The Men in Black were identical in appearance: black suits, pale skin, and seemingly "robotic." Their backs were ramrod straight. They sat motionless with their hands on their knees. To Tonya, they seemed to be more like projections than spirits.

The MIB emitted a weird energy, and Tonya got the impression they were telepathically jamming our equipment to prevent us from communicating with one of the spirits who had been present. Our EVP device stopped working, even though it had a brand-new battery. Tonya tried to communicate with the MIB telepathically, but they were unresponsive.

We use EMF (electromagnetic frequency) meters, which sometimes register spikes in electromagnetic energy when paranormal activity is taking place, or unknown presences manifest. We placed an EMF meter on one of the chairs and it went into the red zone, high activity. The MIBs did not respond – in fact, they didn't respond to anything happening in the room, but seemed singularly focused on our now-jammed EVP device.

We took photographs of the chairs, but nothing registered. In all photographs, the chairs were empty.

Eyewitness drawing of Man In Black seen at the Webb. Credit: Bryon B.

Our investigations at the library usually last for 90 minutes. This time, we stayed longer to see what might develop, but the MIBs did nothing but sit in the chairs with lifeless expressions on their faces. They continued to emit this strange energy that we could not identify. They were still there when we finally had to leave.

The same night, we had our first encounter with the round, hairy being we identified as an interdimensional, and we wondered if there was a connection between it and the MIBs.

We had another investigation two nights later. We hoped to see them again, but they did not return.

Our next encounter was about a week later, when two guest investigators saw the specter of a man cross a hallway and stand by the library's courtyard door. It looked like one of the MIBs. Its presence set off one of the motion sensors. When Tonya aimed her camera at the spot, the face recognition box activated on her phone, but the camera refused to focus. One of the investigators stood where he had seen the MIB. Tonya's cell phone camera worked, but three consecutive photos showed only two streaks of light instead of the investigator. Again, it seemed like something was tampering with our equipment. The figure remained at the courtyard entrance all night, as though it were standing guard.

This time, we were able to run our equipment. We captured some EVPs, which sounded like a deep male voice uttering random phrases and sounds that were impossible to interpret.

We did not see the MIB again until July 5 when we went upstairs to the Cannon Room. The two MIBs were there, but standing instead of sitting. Once again, they were only visible clairvoyantly.

We turned on our equipment and made contact with one of our resident ghosts, the spirit of an African American gambler named Jerry. We have had frequent EVP exchanges with him. Jerry communicated something that sounded like, "(in?)competent" and "guessing." One MIB then attempted to keep Jerry from communicating with us further by grabbing and closing his throat. Tonya summoned angel energy to rescue Jerry. The MIBs then jammed our equipment again. One of them stood with his hands out in a blocking motion in front of the door across the hallway, and the other manifested at the courtyard door. They gave us the impression that they were in control of the library, and did not like us doing investigations.

The same evening, the hairy interdimensional being was seen. We speculated again that it was related to the presence of the MIBs. (The hairy being made appearances on its own as well. Once after it showed

Men In Black at the Library

Possible interdimensional creature see at the Webb. Credit: Tonya Madia.

up, Joey heard it howl like an animal. Oddly, a few days later, the library had to be treated for fleas!)

There were more appearances of the MIB, especially in the Cannon Room. They manifested when Joey was talking about them with another investigator, as though they had been eavesdropping and wanted to let us know they were listening.

The MIBs continued to be seen by other investigators at other times. One of our guest investigators, a sensitive, drew a picture of one he saw. It had Asian features, and the sensitive had not known that some MIBs are Asian in appearance.

Why are MIBs showing up in a haunted library? One reason might be us. We have spent a lot of time investigating in Point Pleasant,

West Virginia, the site of the famous Mothman wave that struck the area in 1966-67. Mothman was a winged humanoid who made a sudden appearance in November 1966, and was seen by hundreds of witnesses over the next 13 months. In addition, there was a marked increase of UFO activity, including lights, craft, landed aliens, poltergeist phenomena and more. We have had experiences in Point Pleasant, including seeing shadow forms, which may be related to MIB, and having missing time. Perhaps we landed on the "MIB radar."

Another reason may be the ongoing UFO activity reported in the vicinity of the library, including around the times we have encountered the MIB.

UFO activity in the area goes back to at least 1955. A hospital, the Morehead City Hospital, once was directly across the street from the library. It later became a nursing home, and now is a hotel. During World War II, the hospital's burn unit was filled with patients. We think some of them, along with later residents of the nursing home, have lingered in the area and haunt the Webb Library.

Tonya discovered that there was a significant UFO sighting above and several blocks from the old hospital on June 30, 1955. It was reported by at least two individuals. Just after dark, the craft was observed flying over the hospital. One of the witnesses was a woman.

According to the NUFORC (National UFO Reporting Center) report:

> *As she was backing out of her parking space she saw a round, saucer-shaped craft approaching from the south (over the water, the Atlantic Ocean). She stated it wasn't very high and made no sound (again, her windows were down at the time). It was low enough that she could easily make out round, what she called "portholes" around the periphery of the saucer. She stated there was yellowish/white light coming from the "portholes." Unsure whether it was actually windows of a sort she was seeing, or if it could have been round lights?[sic] She stated it was moving slowly and silently. It was flying, again, from the southeast to the northwest, over the hospital.*

We have also documented a history of UFO activity in the area, which continues in present times.

All the phenomena – UFOs, ghosts and spirits, interdimensionals and MIB – seem to be interrelated. We have dubbed the upstairs hallway of the library opposite to where the old hospital sat the "Portal Hallway" because of the tremendous amount of activity and communication we have experienced there. The end of the hallway sometimes appears to change dimensions and will at times produce nausea and a feeling of disorientation as if it is being tilted.

One question remains unanswered: what was our ghost friend Jerry trying to communicate to us when the MIB choked him off? Is there something they do not want us to know?

Commentary

Men In Black usually appear in forms that appear solid; however, they can abruptly vanish into thin air. Although they have been documented primarily in UFO-related cases, they also make appearances in paranormal cases. Like other entities and beings associated with the paranormal, UFOs, mysterious creatures and so on, they exhibit paraphysical characteristics. Thus, they are capable of taking a noncorporeal form as they did at the Webb. They were noticed because of the psychic/mediumistic abilities of Tonya Madia and other investigators.

Perhaps more MIB would be noticed if individuals, as well as investigators, developed and used their natural psychic ability, which every person has to some degree. Investigators tend to resist the psychic in the mistaken belief that the only evidence that is significant must be measured on equipment. Thus, they are likely to miss most of the action in many cases.

Our experiences with the phenomena of ufology and the paranormal intersect with alternate realities, and, for a brief span of time, we are neither "here" nor "there," but somewhere in between. We behold things that cannot be explained according to the "rules" of our reality, yet they cannot be denied. As many experiencers state, "I know what I saw."

MIB target both experiencers and investigators, and may make repeated, intimidating visits intended to discourage further activities. The most famous case was one of the earliest documented, Albert K. Bender. In 1952, Bender established the International Flying Saucer Bureau, and a magazine, Space Review, in 1953. He was inspired by his sighting of a UFO over Bridgeport, Connecticut. Supposedly, he discovered the secret of UFOs and announced his plan to reveal all. He was then visited by three MIBs, who he described as shadowy forms that floated above the ground. They told him their forms were an illusion, and they captured humans and used their bodies for disguises. They warned him not to publish anything, and if he did, it would not be believed.

The MIBs somehow took all his notes and documentation, and then initiated a campaign of harassment that included massive headaches and a persistent feeling of being watched. Bender soon folded his bureau.

His story is told in Gray Barker's book, They Knew Too Much About Flying Saucers *(1956)*. Bender published his own account in 1962, Flying Saucers and the Three Men, *in which he opined that his visitors were from another planet. Bender was not the first MIB case on record, but his story established the MIB lore, and provided early evidence for the noncorporeal nature of this mysterious phenomenon.*

There is at least one other account of an MIB visit to a researcher in a library. Peter R. Rojcewicz, a former professor of humanities and folklore at New York's Julliard School, became interested in MIBs and their overlapping folklore with the Devil and other dark figures. One day in 1980, he was at the University of Pennsylvania's library doing research. He was sitting at a table, quietly reading a UFO book recommended to him by another professor. Suddenly, he was confronted by an MIB. He described the encounter in a lecture:

> In the corner of my vision I noticed a black pant leg and a black shoe, scuffed. Standing in front of me was a very gaunt, very pale man. He was about 6-1, weighed about 140 pounds and wore a black suit, black shoes, black string tie and a bright white shirt. His suit was loose, and it looked as though he had slept in it for three days. He sat down, like he had dropped from the ceiling – all in one movement – and folded his hands on top of a stack of books in front of him.

The MIB asked Rojcewicz what he was doing. Peter replied that he was reading a book about flying saucers.
"Have you seen a flying saucer?" the MIB asked.
Rojcewicz said that he had not.
"Do you believe in the reality of flying saucers?"
Rojcewicz said he didn't know much about them and wasn't sure he was very interested in the phenomena.
The MIB screamed, "Flying saucers are the most important fact of the century and you are not interested?"
Peter tried to calm the stranger. The MIB rose in a single awkward movement, put his hand on Rojcewicz's shoulder and said, "Go well on your purpose," and left.
Rojcewicz was instantly overwhelmed by fear. He said:

> I had a sense that this man was out of the ordinary and that idea frightened me. I got up and walked around the stacks toward where the reference librarians usually are. The librarians weren't there. There were no guards there – there was nobody else in the library. I was terrified.
>
> I went back to the table where I had been reading to get myself together. It took me about an hour. Then I got up and everything was back to normal, the people were all there.

He did not talk publicly about his experience for a long time, because he was uncertain how others would react.
Rojcewicz said he knew he had not been dreaming, but felt he had been in an altered state, in some crack in reality. The mysterious lack of people in the library reinforces the idea that MIB and similar experiences – UFOs, alien encounters, paranormal encounters, fairy encounters, and so on – take place in a shifted reality. Had others been around, they most likely would not have seen the MIB – just as the Webb Library MIB were not physically visible to all, but could be seen clairvoyantly to people that they probably select.
The MIB, whoever or whatever they are, target not only UFO witnesses, but others who become interested in UFOs or MIBs and start digging into the mystery. And so it happened to Joey and Tonya Madia.

Appendix 1
J. Allen Hynek on Alien Visitation

J. Allen Hynek (1910-1986) is one of the most famous names in ufology, an investigator and researcher who influenced many prominent figures in the field. An American astronomer, he served as scientific advisor to the U.S. Air Force investigations of UFO reports between 1947 and 1969. The most famous of those was Project Blue Book, which investigated UFOs from a scientific perspective and to determine if they were a threat to national security. After the Condon Report – another scientific study funded by the U.S. Air Force – was published in 1968 stating that there was nothing anomalous about UFOs, Project Blue Book was shut down.

Initially skeptical, Hynek debunked cases, but over time his opinions shifted in the face of unexplained phenomena and credible witnesses. Hynek became disillusioned with the hard line and automatic skepticism of the Air Force and the scientific community.

In the early 1970s, Hynek expressed doubts about the Extraterrestrial Hypothesis – that Earth was being visited by intelligent off-world beings – because of the vast distances of space. By the end of the decade, he said there is evidence for both extraterrestrial and extradimensional (interdimensional) life. He also said that it is possible that a technology existed "which encompasses both the physical and the psychic, the material and the mental" – concepts now being explored today in quantum physics that might explain not only UFOs and aliens, but everything paranormal.

Hynek developed a classification system for encounters. The first three levels are nocturnal lights, daylight discs, and radar-visual objects. The next levels are Close Encounters of the First Kind, a UFO seen in detail less than 500 feet away; Close Encounters of the Second Kind, a UFO event with physical effects, such as to vehicles, witnesses, or the land; and Close Encounters of the Third Kind, in which "animated creatures" are observed in the UFO, such as humanoids, artificial forms, aliens and humans. (Since then, extensions of Hynek's classifications have been added; there are now seven levels.)

The following remarks come from an interview Hynek gave to Michael Brein. His observations still hit the target today. He envisioned aliens communicating not by hard technology, but by the technology of consciousness, through telepathy – a feature of contact documented repeatedly by witnesses, contactees and abductees.

Michael Brein: With the vastness of the universe, would and could aliens travel here?

J. Allen Hynek: It's entirely possible that aliens would travel to visit us, but not very probable, at least from our frame of reference. We have a paradox here. I think it would be absolutely stupid and presumptuous to think that there aren't other forms of life in the universe. It simply is preposterous that with the universe as large as it is, there wouldn't be some other life someplace.

If we made a model of everything that astronomers can see in their telescopes, and we made that model as large as the United States, then to scale, the earth would be so small that it would not be visible even in the world's most powerful electron microscope. It would be sub-microscopic. Wouldn't it be preposterous to think that this sub-microscopic speck on this model would be the only speck in a model as large as the United States to represent the presence of life? It's mind-boggling, inconceivable.

Michael Brein: Why would anybody come here, especially across such apparent vastness?

J. Allen Hynek: Well, that's one of the things against the whole hypothesis of extraterrestrial visitation. We would be hard to find, and the distances that had to be covered would be so great. If there are extraterrestrial visitations, I would think we might get one visit per thousand years.

As it stands, we have several hundred a year reported. It could be that they have a base on one of the moons of Jupiter or something, and make periodic visits here, because it is preposterous to think that every UFO sighting represents a clean-cut visit from way out there. In the same way that we have a base at Antarctica and we launch little expeditions from that, maybe they have bases under the ocean or they have bases on the other side of the moon.

Michael Brein: Why do you think they would come here?

J. Allen Hynek: The human race at its present stage of evolution may have become of interest to intelligences elsewhere. Up to now, for thousands and thousands and thousands of years, we would have been quite uninteresting, just a warring tribe.

If you were examining anthills at various places, and not very often, and then suddenly saw arising from one anthill a totally different social structure – you saw them making instruments of one sort or another – you would get rather interested in that anthill and wonder how their society worked and what was happening.

Now we have SETI, the proposed project of searching for life elsewhere through listening with radio telescopes. There is the proposal that the huge array of radio telescopes called Project Cyclops[1] be built with the express purpose of listening all over the radio spectrum for signs of television programs elsewhere.

Michael Brein: That might be barking up the wrong tree.

J. Allen Hynek: It may very well be barking up the wrong tree, because radios might to other civilizations be as archaic as smoke signals would be

---

[1] Project Cyclops was a 1971 project for directing the Search for Extraterrestrial Intelligence (SETI) arrays of radio telescopes to search for sign of intelligent life up to 1000 light years in distance. It was too expensive to execute but did influence the operation of SETI.

to us. If they purposely wanted to get in touch with us, then maybe they would beam radio signals. But my feeling is that their communication would be much more sophisticated than using radio. They might be using forms of mental telepathy, for instance, to communicate with each other, or they would communicate the way the dolphins do, with sound.

It's certainly worth trying. But wouldn't it be a tremendous and tragic joke on NASA if they spent billions of dollars to try to find microbes on Mars and not one penny was spent to investigate the possibility that life from elsewhere might be right here under our noses – and we're not doing anything about it?

Appendix 2
UFO and Related Organizations

APRO Aerial Phenomena Research Organization, a research group founded by Jim and Coral Lorenzen in 1952, and active until 1988. APRO was well respected for the quality of its investigations, and tapped many scientists as consultants. The APRO files and newsletters are maintained online by Open Minds TV.

CCCS Centre for Crop Circle Studies, founded in the early 1990s by crop circle researchers in England to investigate and study crop circles. A branch was established in the United States. Both became defunct after 2001.

CSETI Center for the Study of Extraterrestrial Intelligence, founded as a nonprofit research organization in 1990 by Steven Greer. Its aim is to "establish peaceful and sustainable relations with extraterrestrial life forms." CSETI also established a new category of encounters, the CE-5 or "close encounters of the fifth kind," defined as human-initiated contact and/or communication with extraterrestrial life.

CUFOS Center for UFO Studies, a privately funded group founded in 1973 by J. Allen Hynek for scientists and academics to pursue scientific investigations of UFOs. When Hynek died in 1986, renamed the J. Allen Hynek Center for UFO Studies. It serves mostly as a library and archives for researchers.

MUFON Mutual UFO Network, a nonprofit organization founded in 1969 by Walter H. Andrus to investigate reports of UFO sightings. It is one of the largest such organizations, with chapters in every state in America and members worldwide.

NARCAP National Aviation and Reporting Center on Anomalous Phenomena, founded in 1999 by Richard Haines, former chief scientist at the NASA Ames Research Center, to collect UFO sightings information from pilots, air traffic controllers, radar operators and other aviation professionals.

NASA While not involved in the ufology field, the National Aeronautics and Space Administration, responsible for civilian manned and unmanned space flights, has collected anomalous data, including videos and photographs of mystery objects in space. NASA, formed in 1958, is an independent agency of the U.S. executive branch.

NICAP National Investigations Committee on Aerial Phenomena, a nonprofit organization founded in 1956 by inventor Thomas Townsend Brown. NICAP was very active into the 1970s and was cited along with APRO by J. Allen Hynek as two of the best civilian UFO groups. It dissolved in 1980 and its files were acquired by CUFOS.

NUFORC National UFO Reporting Center, founded in 1974 by Robert J. Gribble, to investigate UFO sightings and alien contact. It has catalogued about 90,000 UFO sightings, and maintains a 24-hour hotline. Peter Davenport became director in 1994.

SETI The Search for Extraterrestrial Intelligence is a collective term referring to scientific searches for intelligent life in the cosmos. The first modern SETI experiments were done in the 1960s with radio telescopes. Most SETI research has focused on the radio spectrum; lasers and gamma ray bursts have also been considered as means of communication. Various SETI projects have been funded, including by NASA. A nonprofit SETI Institute was founded in 1984 by Carl Sagan and Jill Tartar.

About the Authors

Michael Brein

Michael Brein is an author, lecturer, consultant, travel storyteller, adventurer, and publisher of travel books and guides. He earned his PhD in social psychology, with a specialty in psychology—all things travel—as well as an MBA at the University of Hawaii. He has had a career for more than 20 years as a college professor in psychology and business, teaching at a variety of universities in Hawaii, as well as an overseas two-year stint teaching for the University of Maryland in Europe.

Michael was the first to coin the term "travel psychology." Through his doctoral studies, work, life experiences and world travels, he became the world's first and perhaps only travel psychologist. As "The Travel Psychologist," he appears in leading newspapers, magazines, blogs, and radio programs all over the world, commenting on the psychology of travel.

Michael has been a member of a number of world travel clubs including the Travelers Century Club, whose requirement for membership is travel to a minimum of 100 countries, and the Circumnavigators Club, which requires going around the world in one complete trip.

He was the first to complete the United Airlines "50 State Marathon" contest in 1985, flying to all 50 U.S. states to win a first-class pass for a year on United's domestic U.S. flights, including Hawaii.

Michael's travel guide series, *Michael Brein's Travel Guides to Sightseeing by Public Transportation*, is a first of its kind, showing travelers how to sightsee the top 50 visitor attractions in the world's most popular cities easily and cheaply by public transportation.

Michael has traveled the world over for the last four decades interviewing nearly 1,800 world travelers and adventurers, collecting their fantastic travel stories for an ebook and audiobook series on the psychology of travel.

Michael resides on Bainbridge Island, Washington. His website is www.michaelbrein.com, and email is michaelbrein@gmail.com.

Rosemary Ellen Guiley

Rosemary Ellen Guiley is one of the leading figures in the paranormal and metaphysical fields: author, researcher, investigator, and publisher. She has written more than 65 nonfiction books on a wide range of topics, including a series of authoritative single-volume encyclopedias. She is often the "go-to" person for explanations of unusual phenomena and events.

Her work focuses on the how and why people have extraordinary experiences of all kinds: paranormal, spiritual and mystical, contact with the dead, contact with aliens and otherworldly beings, and psychic breakthroughs.

Rosemary owns and runs an independent publishing house, Visionary Living, Inc., which publishes paranormal, metaphysical and ufology titles. She also publishes *Strange Dimensions*, a monthly newsletter and blog. She is Executive Editor of *FATE* magazine.

Rosemary has served on the board and the research committee of the Edgar Mitchell Foundation for Research Into Extraterrestrial Encounters. She is a founding member of the Afterlife Research and Education Institute, and a fellow of the International Institute for Integral Human Sciences in Montreal.

Rosemary makes numerous media appearances and lectures internationally. She is a frequent guest on *Coast to Coast AM* with George Noory. She lives in Connecticut.

Her website is www.visionaryliving.com, and her email is reguiley@gmail.com.

Afterword

We hope you enjoyed our second collection of unusual travel tales, not only out on the open Earth road, but into other dimensions as well.

We are planning more volumes, and we'd like to hear from you. We're interested in travel experiences involving paranormal phenomena; ghosts and hauntings; visions; psychic experiences; time slips; past lives; déjà vu; synchronicity; mysterious creatures and beings; UFOs and aliens; crop circles; sacred sites, mystical experiences; and more.

Stories can be of any length. We reserve the right to edit them to fit the style and format of our books. Stories will be credited to the authors. As a thank you, we will send you an autographed print copy of the book.

Please send your stories to either Michael Brein at michaelbrein@gmail.com or Rosemary Ellen Guiley at reguiley@gmail.com.

Meanwhile, check out our first Road collection, *The Road to Strange: Travel Tales of the Paranormal and Beyond*, available on Amazon.

Thank you and happy travels, wherever they may take you!

www.ingramcontent.com/pod-product-compliance
Lightning Source LLC
Chambersburg PA
CBHW021142080526
44588CB00008B/182